MALINALLI

FLOWERSONG
PRESS

Book and Lyrics
by
Robert Paul Moreira

Music .
by
Robert Paul Moreira and Josiah Esquivel

FLOWERSONG
P R E S S

FlowerSong Press
Copyright © 2022 by Robert Paul Moreira and Josiah Esquivel
ISBN: 978-1-953447-66-1
Library of Congress Control Number: 2022934891

Published by FlowerSong Press
in the United States of America.
www.flowersongpress.com

Cover Art by Mario Godinez
Cover Design by Edward Vidaurre

NOTICE: SCHOOLS AND BUSINESSES
FlowerSong Press offers copies of this book at quantity
discount with bulk purchase for educational, business,
or sales promotional use. For information, please email
the Publisher at info@flowersongpress.com.

Table of Contents

Special Thanks

With special permission from Aunt Lute Press, "Goddess" lyrics include excerpts from Gloria Anzaldúa's *Borderlands/La Frontera/The New Mestiza*, 3rd Edition.

Also, my sincerest gratitude to Denisse Zecca for her editorial assistance.

Author's Note

The road to the *Malinalli* script and musical selections you hold in your hands began when, under the sponsorship of Dr. Marci McMahon and the Mexican American Studies Program at the University of Texas Pan American (now UT Rio Grande Valley), selections from the musical were performed by students as *Azteca Unplugged* during the 2014 Festival of International Books and Arts at UTRGV. Three years, several revisions, and one doctoral dissertation later, Dr. McMahon would once again help me develop the musical further by introducing me to Josiah Esquivel, then a Music major at UTRGV. I can honestly say that working with Josiah has been one of the most rewarding experiences of my life, as without his expertise the music of *Malinalli* would never have matured. Because of their patience, guidance, expertise and above all friendship, I am indebted to both Dr. McMahon and Josiah; without them, *Malinalli* would not be what it is today.

Since meeting Josiah, *Malinalli* has been workshopped several times at UTRGV, and to great success. With the generous support of a number of university agencies, including the College of Fine Arts, the B3 Institute, and the Office of Global Engagement every workshop was directed and performed by students. To all the students who participated in the workshops throughout the years, including *Azteca Unplugged*: This book is as much for Josiah and I as it is for you. My sincerest thanks for helping shape *Malinalli*.

Lastly, to Edward Vidaurre and FlowerSong Press: *Bravo!* for venturing outside of your publication "comfort zone" to take on a project like *Malinalli*. Josiah and I could not have found a more perfect home for our words and music.

— **Robert Paul Moreira**

Preface:

'Beware the Goddess!':
Re-Staging Malinalli/La Malinche

by Marci R. McMahon

The woman who defies her role as subservient to her husband, father, brother, or son […] is purported to be a traitor to her race by contributing to the genocide of her people […] she is *una Malinchista*. Like the Malinche of Mexican history, she is corrupted by foreign influences, which threaten to destroy her people.[1]

Malintzin's history, her legend and subsequent mythic dimensions as evil goddess and creator of a new race – the mestizo race, embroils her in a family quarrel, where many male members often prefer to see her as the mother-whore, bearer of illegitimate children, responsible for the foreign Spanish invasion; and where the female members attempt to restore balance in ways that are sometimes painfully ambivalent, and at other times attempt to topple the traditional patriarchal mythology through revision and re-vision.[2]

After the conquest of Tabasco, a province located on the Yucatán coast, Hernán Cortés received from the ruling Mayan chiefs a gift of twenty maidens who were to essentially serve as domestic laborers for the Spanish conquistadores. One of these maidens was the fourteen-year old Malinal, christened by the Spaniards as "Marina," who later earned the honorific title '-*tzin*, thus Malintzin, and later known as La Malinche.[3] As the history goes, La Malinche quickly distinguished herself among the other maidens for her ability to serve the conquistadores so well through translation.[4] With the power of language, Malintzin aided Cortés with translations and counsel whenever he confronted enemies or met with indigenous allies. Bernal Díaz del Castillo, Cortés's confidant, claims that without Malintzin, the Spaniards could not have understood the language of Mexico – and thus as contemporary scholars perceive it he could not have accomplished the Spanish conquest. As Cortés's mistress, Malintzin also gave birth to their son, Martín, and thus purportedly gave birth to the first *mestizo*.[5]

For her role as translator, negotiator, cultural mediator, and mistress to Cortés, La Malinche remains an immensely controversial figure. By the twentieth century in Mexico, her name was synonymous with conquest, and the word *malinche* or *malinchista* today in Mexico connotes a person who is a traitor to his or her country.[6] In Chicanx nationalist discourse, La Malinche has been configured as both whore and traitor for "selling out" her people to the Spaniards.[7] As Cherríe Moraga states in the first epigraph to this Preface, dominant histories of La Malinche have configured Malintzin as a traitor to her race, silencing her role as an active negotiator. And because of this legacy, contemporary Chicanas who dare critique patriarchal, community, and nationalist structures are often viewed as *malinchistas*.[8] Norma Alarcón's quote in the second epigraph uses the framework of family to explain La Malinche's betrayal. In Alarcón's narrative, La Malinche is constantly "embroiled" in a "family quarrel" with the men of the family who perceive her as both mother (La Virgen de Guadalupe) and whore, and often entangled by the female members of the family who desire to appropriate La Malinche as a powerful female icon and resistor to colonization and patriarchy.

In several respects, La Malinche was a "domestic negotiator" – between the nations of Spain and Mexico, between the Spaniards and indigenous, and within her own domestic sphere as laborer and mistress to Cortés.[9] Her acts of negotiation can be gleaned from her strategic use of language, intuition, and knowledge, which subsequently enabled her to survive the conquest during her lifetime and not fall victim to the rule of the Spanish conquistador. Such modes of negotiation enabled La Malinche to survive the fate offered to her by historical circumstances and her family who sold her into slavery. In this light, La Malinche becomes a powerful icon of female agency and negotiator to the patriarchal and nationalist structures that sought to marginalize and demonize her.

Cultural productions that seek to represent the controversial figure of La Malinche must wrestle with Malinalli's controversial history and complex role in the Spanish conquest. Robert Paul Moreira and Josiah Esquivel's musical *Malinalli* follows in the Chicana feminist tradition of re-telling and restaging the dynamic history of La Malinche because the work imbues the iconic figure with agency and power. I have had the privilege of witnessing Moreira and Esquivel's musical in its different iterations, including *Azteca Unplugged* (2014), *Malinalli, Act I* (2018), *Malinalli, Act II* (2018), and *Malinalli: the Complete Musical* (2019). In each of these productions, Moreira and Esquivel worked with students at The University of Texas Rio Grande Valley (UTRGV) to develop a dynamic musical with staging, vocal performance, and sound design, portraying Malinalli's domestic negotiations. In Moreira and Esquivel's *Malinalli*, audiences witness the female figure's transformation as mistress and pawn in Cortez's conquest to a leader of her people who by the curtain's closing proclaims: "We are the Goddess!" Not only does the character Malinalli have the last words at the musical's end, but she leaves audiences with a transformative message: women and other marginalized communities are not victims, but are active mediators with the ability to transform their fates.

In the same way that Moreira and Esquivel's *Malinalli* depicts the figure of La Malinche as a force of cultural mediation, the hybrid musical captures the mestizaje of the Américas on both sides of the U.S.-Mexico border. With music developed by Moreira and Esquivel, *Malinalli*'s score and soundscape draws on Western musical traditions, including elements of the Broadway musical, with a soundscape reminiscent of rock opera's such as Andrew Lloyd Webber's 1970 *Jesus Chris Superstar* (lyrics by Tim Rice) and iconic rock albums such as Jethro Tull's 1971 *Aqualung*. At the same time, *Malinalli* subverts the Western musical form by bringing in hybrid Latin American instrumentation, such as the clave and flute, evoking Indigenous and Afro-Caribbean sounds. In this way, *Malinalli*'s soundscape follows in the tradition of the few Latinx musicals produced on Broadway; here, Lin-Manuel Miranda's 2008 *In the Heights* (book by Quiara Alegría-Hudes). *Malinalli's* soundscape thus embodies La Malinche's role as cultural and linguistic mediator.

The excitement by UTRGV students and the Rio Grande Valley community as Moreira and Esquivel developed *Malinalli* from 2014-2019 speaks volumes to the necessity of Latinx theatrical works on stages in the South Texas Rio Grande Valley region and nation. Throughout moments of social injustice, Latinx theatrical works such as *Malinalli* continue to play an integral role in documenting histories of oppression and resistance by creating new soundscapes, ways of speaking, musical styles, and performance traditions. Moreira and Esquivel's *Malinalli* adds to this tradition by countering white supremacist rhetoric that seeks to repress the vocality of diverse bodies. As public performances of white supremacy continued to spread across the U.S., Latinx stories on public stages across the U.S. are urgent now more than ever. Indeed, as Malinalli powerfully proclaims and warns audiences by the end of the musical: "Beware the Goddess!"

---

[1] Cherríe Moraga, *Loving in the War Years: Lo que nunca pasó por sus labios* (Cambridge: South End Press, 1983) 113.

[2] Norma Alarcón, "Chicana's Feminist Literature: A Re-Vision Through Malintzin/or Malintzin: Putting Flesh Back on the Object," *This Bridge Called My Back: Writings by Radical Women of Color*, eds. Cherríe Moraga and Gloria Anzaldúa (New York: Kitchen Table: Women of Color Press, 1981) 182.

[3] La Malinche is thought to have been named Malinal after "Malinalli," the day of her birth, which was the custom at the time. She was named "Marina" by the Spaniards and even given the Spanish title of respect "doña." Similar honor was given to her by the Mayan rulers who addressed her by the standard honorific title, -tzin. According to Cordelia Candelaria, the development of "Malinche" from Malintzin seems to be purely a linguistic phenomenon. Cordelia Candelaria, "La Malinche: Feminist Prototype," *Frontiers: A Journal of Women Studies*, 5. 2 (Summer 1980): 2.

[4] As the daughter of an Aztec chief, La Malinche was a member of a privileged, educated class, most likely where she became fluent in both Mayan and Nahuatl. During this period, Spanish was translated to Maya and then to Nahuatl. Furthermore, after her father's death and mother's subsequent re-marriage, Malinche was sold into slavery. Malintzin was sold into slavery by her mother because after her husband's death, Malintzin's mother wanted to gain control of her daughter's inheritance so that she could bear a son for her second husband. Candelaria, 2.

[5] *Mestizo* denotes a person of mixed Spanish and indigenous ancestry.

[6] Tey Diana Rebolledo and Eliana S. Rivero, eds. *Infinite Divisions: An Anthology of Chicana Literature* (Tucson: University of Arizona Press, 1993) 191.

[7] La Malinche's sexual relationship with Cortés, amidst all other acts, has been configured as her ultimate betrayal. Gloria Anzaldúa, *Borderlands/La Frontera: The New Mestiza*, 3rd edition (San Francisco: Aunt Lute Books, 1987) 44.

[8] This was the term directed at Chicanas who focused on feminist issues during the Chicano Movement.

[9] See Marci R. McMahon, *Domestic Negotiations: Gender, Nation, and Self-Fashioning in US Mexicana and Chicana Literature and Art.* New Jersey: Rutgers University Press, 2013.

Malinalli

The Script

Production History

Azteca Unplugged, directed by Robert Paul Moreira, was performed in the Library Auditorium at the University of Texas Rio Grande Valley in March of 2014. Performers included Pamela Matias, Alejandra Rocha, John Medalla, David Hernandez, Brianna Tapia, Carolina Garcia, Beatriz Ramirez, Juan Flores, Jr., Mark Lopez, Cecilia Rivera, and Hilda Ortiz.

Malinalli, Act I, directed by Jasmine Grimaldo, received a concert workshop in the Library Auditorium at UT Rio Grande Valley on May 5, 2018.

Cast

Malinalli..........Princess Chavez
Teuhtliltzin..........Paolo Santiago
Moctezuma..........Rogelio Zamora
Hernán Cortéz..........Oscar Camacho
Juan Jaramillo..........Mark Peña
Juan Velásquez de León..........Jose Garcia
Diego de Ordaz..........Jennifer Saenz
Cuauhtémoc..........Mihir Shah

Malinalli, Act II, directed by Michaela Gomez and Nallely Pitones, received a concert workshop in the Student Union Theater at UT Rio Grande Valley on December 6, 2018.

Cast

Malinalli..........Princess Chavez
Teuhtliltzin..........Michael Lucio
Moctezuma..........Emmanuel Vargas
Hernán Cortéz..........Ronnie Zamora
Juan Jaramillo..........Mark Peña
Juan Velásquez de León..........Joseph Esquivel
Diego de Ordaz..........Jackelyn Cortez
Tecuichpo..........Destinee Rae Lopez
Cuauhtémoc..........Paolo Santiago

Malinalli, the Complete Musical, directed by Brianna Ramirez and Daniela Lozano, was workshopped in the Jeffers Theater at UT Rio Grande Valley on May 2, 2019.

Cast

Malinalli..........Mandy Carin
Teuhtliltzin..........Javier Robles
Moctezuma..........Christopher Treviño
Hernán Cortéz..........Alex Torres
Juan Jaramillo..........Paulina Longoria
Juan Velásquez de León..........Jessie Anaya
Diego de Ordaz..........Pedro Cano
Tecuichpo..........Destinee Rae Lopez
Cuauhtémoc..........Ruben Quintero

Malinalli

by
Robert Paul Moreira and Josiah Esquivel

CAST OF CHARACTERS (in order of appearance)

MALINALLI	Late teens; Mayan princess
TEUHTLILTZIN	40s; Male; Aztec advisor
MOCTEZUMA	30s; Male; Aztec emperor
HERNÁN CORTÉZ	30s; Spanish Conquistador
JUAN JARAMILLO	30s; HIS friend
JUAN VELÁSQUEZ DE LEÓN	30s; Conquistador
DIEGO DE ORDAZ	50s; Conquistador
TECUICHPO	Late teens; MOCTEZUMA's daughter
CUAUHTÉMOC	20s; MOCTEZUMA's nephew
CREW, AZTECS, NOBLES, and TOTONACS	

TIME / SETTING

1502 thru 1521.
Cuba and Tenochtitlán, capital city of the Aztecs.

ACT I

Scene 1: Intersection of Space and Time.
Scene 2: Cuba, 1519. The home of HERNÁN CORTÉZ.
Scene 3: MOCTEZUMA's Palace in Tenochtitlán.

ACT II

Scene 1: Intersection of Space and Time.
Scene 2: MOCTEZUMA's Palace, 1520.
Scene 3: A Garden in Tenochtitlán.

Song List

Act I

01. Overture/Goddess
02. Welcome to Tenochtitlán
03. We Vote for Moctezuma
04. Somewhere
05. Crimson Tide
06. Judgment Day
07. Veracruz, 1519
08. Do It For Your Crew
09. Does Your Emperor Have Gold?
10. Hernán Cortéz
11. What Will Happen To Us?
12. Zenzontle
13. You Will Love Me
14. The Deal
15. All You Need To Do
16. The Deal (Reprise)
17. Promises

Act II

18. The Story You Will Know
19. Tecuichpo's Prayer
20. Welcome to Tenochtitlán (Reprise)
21. The Ball Game/Obsidian Blade
22. You're What I've Been Waiting For
23. Betrayals
24. Gods and Men
25. World of a Difference
26. One Thing I Must Tell You
27. La Noche Triste
28. The Song Will Go On
29. In His Arms
30. Tlakatilistli (The Birth)
31. Jaguar and Ocelot
32. Ollintonatiuh (Fifth Sun)
33. Goddess (Finale)

SYNOPSIS

Act I

Through Space and Time, MALINALLI conjures her life story **(Overture/Goddess)**.

1502, in the ancient city of Tenochtitlán, the AZTECS and TEUHTLILTZIN prepare to choose the successor to the deceased emperor **(Welcome to Tenochtitlán)**. Despite Teuhtliltzin's protests, MOCTEZUMA is appointed the new emperor of the Aztec empire **(We Vote for Moctezuma)**.

1519, Cuba. As he prepares for a new expedition, HERNÁN CORTÉZ writes a letter to his wife, Catalina **(Somewhere)**. Cortéz joins JUAN JARAMILLO, JUAN VELÁSQUEZ DE LEÓN, DIEGO DE ORDAZ, and CREW before departing for the New World **(Crimson Tide)**. León secretly confesses his love for Catalina, and his hatred for Cortéz **(Judgment Day)**.

Months later, Cortéz and company arrive in ancient Veracruz **(Veracruz, 1519)**, where they are immediately accosted by Teuhtliltzin and the TOTONACS, a tribe enslaved by the Aztecs. Ordaz produces Malinalli and reveals her ability to speak both Spanish and Nahuatl, the language of the Aztecs. He pressures Cortéz into forcing Malinalli to ask Teuhtliltzin for more riches **(Do It For Your Crew)**. Cortéz renames Malinalli "Marina," gifts her a rosary, and employs her as translator **(Does Your Emperor Have Gold?)**. Mesmerized by Cortéz, Malinalli sings of her newfound emotions for the Spanish captain **(Hernán Cortéz)**.

In Tenochtitlán weeks later, after hearing of Cortéz, an older Moctezuma questions the future of his empire now that the god Cortéz-Quetzalcóatl has returned **(What Will Happen To Us?)**. TECUICHPO struggles with the reality of marrying her cousin CUAUHTÉMOC (Zenzontle). Cuauhtémoc vows to make Tecuichpo love him **(You Will Love Me)**.

Teuhtliltzin secretly returns to Veracruz and reveals his ambitions to Malinalli **(The Deal)**. Malinalli and Cortéz comfort each other **(All You Need To Do)**.

Back in Tenochtitlán, despite Cuauhtémoc's protests, Teuhtliltzin convinces Moctezuma to welcome Cortéz to the Aztec capital **(The Deal (Reprise))**. In the finale to Act I **(Promises)**, Ordaz urges León to wait a bit longer before killing Cortéz; Teuhtliltzin revels in the prospect of dethroning Moctezuma; Malinalli vows to help Cortéz; Cortéz persuades his crew to march into Tenochtitlán; Cuauhtémoc and Tecuichpo wrestle with their futures; Moctezuma submits to his people and agrees to welcome these long-lost gods into Tenochtitlán.

ACT 2

Through Space and Time, Malinalli continues her story **(The Story You Will Know)**. Weeks later in Tenochtitlán, Tecuichpo makes an offering to the gods and declares her dreams **(Tecuichpo's Prayer)**.

Cortéz, Malinalli, and Spaniards finally arrive at the causeway to Tenochtitlán, where Teuhtliltzin convinces Moctezuma to let the "gods" in **(Welcome to Tenochtitlán (Reprise))**. Cuauhtémoc resists and immediately challenges Cortéz to the sacred game of tlachtli, losing on purpose in order to force Cortéz into a performance of human sacrifice **(The Ball Game/Obsidian Blade)**. Wise to the plan and fearing for Cortéz's life, Malinalli chooses not to translate, and because of this Cortéz rebukes her. Teuhtliltzin quickly intercedes, denying Cuauhtémoc his victory, and he orders Tecuichpo to lead Cortéz to his temple. Touring Tenochtitlán, Cortéz and Tecuichpo fall in love and kiss **(You're What I've Been Waiting For)**. Witnessing this from the shadows, Malinalli rips off the rosary and vows to destroy Cortéz **(Betrayals)**.

After contemplating the arrival of Cortéz, Moctezuma abandons his headdress and abdicates the Aztec throne **(Gods and Men)**.

Weeks later, now under the rule of Emperor Teuhtliltzin, León and Ordaz oversee the enslaved, sickly Aztecs as they bring forth gold and riches, while Cuauhtémoc vows to fight back **(World of a Difference)**.

Malinalli returns in disguise to confront Teuhtliltzin. She betrays Cortéz by revealing her pregnancy **(One Thing I Must Tell You)**. Moctezuma reclaims the Aztec throne as both Teuhtliltzin and Malinalli escape.

On the other side of Tenochtitlán and tired of waiting, León finally confronts Cortéz, just as Moctezuma, Cuauhtémoc, and the Aztecs attack **(La Noche Triste)**. To save Cortéz's life, Jaramillo kills Moctezuma, and the guilt is too much for him to bear **(The Song Will Go On)**.

In separate parts of the Aztec world, Malinalli and Tecuichpo sing of their tragic love for Cortéz **(In His Arms)**. Unimpressed, Cuauhtémoc forces Tecuichpo to marry him.

Malinalli births the first mestizo, Martín Cortéz **(Tlakatilistli (The Birth))**.

Teuhtliltzin finds and confronts Malinalli. He attempts to steal her child, but must first pay back the ghosts his ambitions created **(Jaguar and Ocelot)**.

1521; Tenochtitlán is in ruins, with death all around, and the Spaniards victorious **(Ollintonatiuh (Fifth Sun))**. In the desolation, Malinalli seeks out Cortéz to show him the child. Cortéz steals the child away. Through Space and Time and multiple voices, Malinalli's child is returned to her and her story (re)constituted **(Goddess (Finale))**.

SCENE 1

SETTING: At the intersection of Space
                                     and Time.

AT RISE:

                    (Darkness. Spotlight on MALINALLI,
                      late teens, centerstage.)

1. **OVERTURE/GODDESS**

                         MALINALLI
        THEY SAY I BETRAYED MY PEOPLE
        THEY SAY I'M THE ONE TO BLAME
        THAT I ADDED INJURY TO INSULT
        WHEN THE SPANIARDS CAME

        THEY SAY THAT I BROUGHT THE END
        WHEN I MADE CORTÉZ MY FRIEND
        THAT I OFFERED HIM MY HAND
        AND HE CRUSHED TENOCHTITLÁN

        YOU KNOW I COULD HAVE BEEN A PRINCESS
        BUT MY FATHER DIED FIGHTING THE AZTECS
        THEN MY MOTHER CHOSE A MAN
        HAD A SON AND I WAS SHUNNED AWAY

        WHEN YOUR MOTHER GIVES YOU AWAY
        AND YOU GET SOLD OFF AS A SLAVE
        THEN CORTÉZ ARRIVES-TAKES YOU IN HIS STRIDE
        AND YOU HELP HIM COMMUNICATE
        UNTIL LOVE GETS IN THE WAY

        JUST LIKE THE GODDESS
        CUT INTO PIECES
        YOU'RE ROBBED OF ALL THAT IS DIVINE
        FOR JUST THE CRIME OF BEING BORN

JUST LIKE THE GODDESS
WON'T RULE OUT VENGEANCE
YOU GIRD YOUR DREAMS AND BIDE YOUR TIME
UNTIL THE DAY YOU WILL TRANSFORM
INTO THE GODDESS

HISTORY YOU ARE THE LIES
THAT MEN HAVE WROUGHT
CORTÉZ SAILED OFF WITH THE SPOILS
BUT IT WAS I WHO WON

I GAZED WITH LOVE
AT THE SERPENT'S TENDER FACE
I PAID THE PRICE FOR US ALL
THE NEW COSMIC RACE

OH, NOW I COME THROUGH SPACE AND TIME
NOW AS THE MOON AND STARS ALIGN

JUST LIKE THE GODDESS
CUT INTO PIECES
I GATHER ALL THAT IS DIVINE
LIMBS, HEART, AND SOUL
I AM REBORN

JUST LIKE THE GODDESS
NOT LIKE YOUR JESUS
I DEAL THE WRATH INSIDE THE STORM
BEHOLD, MALINCHE, BUT TRANSFORMED
INTO THE GODDESS!
BEWARE THE GODDESS!
I AM THE GODDESS!

      (Pause. SHE approaches the
      Audience.)

                MALINALLI
AND SO THIS CURSE
THIS TRAGEDY AGAIN
IT'S ALL I HAVE
MY MEMORIES OF HIM

AND EVERYTIME
YOU BLAME ME FOR MY CRIME
I LIVE MY STORY
ONE MORE TIME...

> (SHE fades and exits. Lights rise.
> The stage transforms into
> Tenochtitlán, the capital city of
> the Aztec empire in ancient Mexico,
> 1502. The Great Pyramid is in the
> background, atop which sits a
> statue of the god Quetzalcoatl. A
> new day begins in Tenochtitlán as
> AZTECS flood the stage.)

2. <u>WELCOME TO TENOCHTITLÁN</u>

AZTECS

WELCOME TO TENOCHTITLÁN
WE ARE THE PEOPLE OF THE SUN
THIS IS WHERE THE EAGLE ATE THE SNAKE
THAT IS WHY WE CHOSE TO SETTLE ON THIS LAKE

WELCOME TO TENOCHTITLÁN
WE ARE THE AZTEC NATION
WE ARE THE UNKNOWN CIVILIZATION
THE BEST KEPT SECRET OF THE NEW WORLD

LONG AGO WE LEFT AZTLÁN
AND WE FOUND OUR PROMISED LAND
JUST LIKE MECCA TO THE AZTECA
TENOCHTITLÁN

WELCOME TO TENOCHTITLÁN
HOME TO THE MEXICA
WE HAVE SUBJUGATED EVERY TRIBE AROUND
WHEREVER YOU TURN TO LOOK WE OWN THE TOWN

THE WESTERN SOCIETY
NO ONE ELSE AROUND COMPETES
WE ARE THE SOVEREIGN CLAN AND THIS IS OUR LAND

TENOCHTITLÁN

NO PLACE LIKE TENOCHTITLÁN
CITY UNDERNEATH THE SUN
CHAMPION CITY--WHERE EVERYONE WANTS TO BE
TENOCHTITLÁN

> (Music continues in the midst of
> ordinary Aztec life: children
> tossing rubber balls back and
> forth; artisans chipping away at a
> large piece of stone destined to become
> the famous Aztec Sun Stone; women
> braiding the hair of THEIR daughters;
> merchants bartering; a group
> experiencing *atole*, corn paste,
> for the first time.)

> (TEUHTLILTZIN, 40s, enters.)

TEUHTLILTZIN
WELCOME TO TENOCHTITLÁN
I'VE WAITED FOR THIS DAY SO LONG
TODAY IS THE DAY I PRAY THE GODS WILL FAVOR ME
TODAY IS THE DAY WE CHOOSE A NEW KING

AHUITZOTL'S DEAD AND GONE
I COULD BE NEXT ON THE THRONE
I COULD RULE TENOCHTITLÁN
NO PLACE GIVES A MAN THIS CHANCE THAT I HAVE ONLY
TENOCHTITLÁN

AZTECS
NO PLACE LIKE TENOCHTITLÁN
BIGGER THAN TEOTIHUACÁN
JUST LIKE MECCA TO THE AZTECA
TENOCHTITLÁN

AZTEC GROUP #1	AZTEC GROUP #2
NO PLACE LIKE TENOCHTITLÁN	THE WESTERN METROPOLIS
BIGGER THAN TEOTIHUACÁN	NO ONE ELSE AROUND COMPETES
JUST LIKE MECCA	WE ARE THE SOVEREIGN CLAN

TO THE AZTECA   AND THIS IS OUR LAND
TENOCHTITLÁN   TENOCHTITLÁN

AZTEC GROUP #1
NO PLACE LIKE TENOCHTITLÁN!

AZTEC GROUP #2
OUR NEW KING IS NOW AT HAND!

TEUHTLILTZIN
GODS ABOVE, AM I THE ONE?

AZTECS
NOW OUR NEW TLATOANI WILL COME!

AZTECS & TEUHTLILTZIN
WELCOME TO TENOCHTITLÁN!

(A conch shell sounds, followed by
drums.)

AZTEC 1
Hail Moctezuma, Captain General of our great empire!

(MOCTEZUMA, 30s and battle-scarred,
enters. AZTECS bow THEIR heads.
NOBLES enter and gather around
TEUHTLILTZIN and MOCTEZUMA.)

3. WE VOTE FOR MOCTEZUMA

NOBLE 1
LET US GET TO THE BUSINESS AT HAND
FROM AMONG THESE WE MUST CHOOSE ONE MAN
HE NEEDS TO BE WISE
HE NEEDS TO BE BRAVE
HE MUST BE A KING
AND NOT A SLAVE

NOBLE 2
YES, HE MUST BE SHREWD AND HE MUST STAND
LIKE THE GREATEST EMPEROR OF THE LAND

                    NOBLES 3 & 4
BUT WHO IS IT
AMONG THESE TWO
THAT'S THE BEST?
WHOM DO WE CHOOSE?

                    NOBLES 1 & 2
WE VOTE FOR MOCTEZUMA
HE'S GOT WHAT WE WANT
HE'S BRAVE AND STRONG
THE PERFECT KING FOR US ALL
MOCTEZUMA, HE'S OUR MAN

YOU SHOULD VOTE FOR MOCTEZUMA
HE'S GOT WHAT WE ALL WANT
THE BLOOD IN HIS VEINS
HIS UNCLE HAD IN HIS DAYS
MOCTEZUMA, HE'S OUR MAN

                    TEUHTLILTZIN
DON'T GET ME WRONG
I'M SURE YOU HAVE REASONS
BUT BLOOD'S NOT ENOUGH
IN MY BOOK TO BE KING

MOCTEZUMA'S A KID
AND NOT WHAT THE PEOPLE NEED
CHOOSE A MAN THAT CAN
STAND HIS GROUND LIKE ME

                    MOCTEZUMA
TO BE KING IS A GREAT RESPONSIBILITY
BUT I'M MORE THAN THE BOY YOU ALL SEE
I'VE FOUGHT IN WARS AND BROUGHT US GLORY
I'VE FOUGHT BESIDE HUITZILOPOCHTLI

                    NOBLE 3
                    (to MOCTEZUMA)
GRAND SPEECH BUT I DO NOT AGREE
YOU ARE JUST TOO YOUNG TO LEAD

                        NOBLES 1 & 2
                     (to NOBLES 3 & 4)
        BUT ALL HE'S DONE--

                        NOBLES 3 & 4
                     (in rebuttal)
        TEUHTLILTZIN DID WHEN HE WAS YOUNG!

                        NOBLES 1 & 2
        HE'S NEXT IN BLOOD!

                        NOBLES 3 & 4
        HE'S NEXT TO RULE CEM ANÁHUAC!

                        NOBLES & AZTECS
        AND WE THOUGHT WE'D GET TO LEAVE BY NOON!

                        TEUHTLILTZIN
                     (to NOBLES 3 & 4, over
                     music)
        By Tlaloc, look at them! We had a deal. You promised they would
        choose me!

                        NOBLE 3
        They want blood, Teuhtliltzin. And you don't have it.

                        NOBLES 1 & 2
                     (to AZTECS)
        Ladies and gentlemen, do not forget that Moctezuma returns to
        us victorious as well! An Eagle Warrior, just like our late
        great emperor, Ahuitzotl!

                     (The AZTECS cheer. TEUHTLILTZIN
                     sees HIS chances slipping away.)

                        TEUHTLILTZIN
        No!
            CHOOSE ME!
            TO RULE IS MY DESTINY!

                         MOCTEZUMA
CHOOSE ME!
TENOCHTITLÁN NEEDS ME!

                         TEUHTLILTZIN
                       (desperately)
CHOOSE ME
CHOOSE WHAT YOU REALLY NEED

THIS IS LUNACY
CAN'T YOU SEE
WHAT WILL OCCUR
IF YOU LET HIM BECOME
OUR NEW TLATOANI?

                    NOBLES 1, 2 & AZTECS
TEUHTLILTZIN
YOU MUST SEE
YOU CAN'T
COMPETE WITH HIM

                    NOBLES 3 & 4
LET'S TAKE A VOTE!

                    NOBLES 1, 2 & AZTECS
OH, WHAT FOR?
WE KNOW WHO IT MUST BE

          (NOBLES 1 & 2 push TEUHTLILTZIN
           aside, bring forth MOCTEZUMA. The
           AZTECS cheer.)

                    NOBLES 1, 2 & AZTECS
WE VOTE FOR MOCTEZUMA
HE'S GOT WHAT WE ALL WANT
HE'S BRAVE AND STRONG
THE PERFECT KING FOR US ALL
MOCTEZUMA, HE'S OUR MAN

          (To TEUHTLILTZIN's chagrin, NOBLES
           3 & 4 concede and join in the
           celebration.)

NOBLES & AZTECS
WE VOTE FOR MOCTEZUMA
HE'S GOT WHAT WE ALL WANT
THE BLOOD IN HIS VEINS
HIS UNCLE HAD IN HIS DAYS
IT'S ONLY FITTING IT'S YOUR
UNCLE YOU SHOULD SUCCEED
MOCTEZUMA, YOU'RE OUR MAN!

TEUHTLILTZIN
SO CLOSE, NOW SO FAR AWAY
HE WILL PAY
TODAY WAS MY DAY
MOCTEZUMA!

TEUHTLILTZIN
MOCTEZUMA, YOU ARE DAMNED!

NOBLES & AZTECS
MOCTEZUMA, YOU'RE OUR MAN!

(The AZTECS bring forth a pair of
golden sandals and a brilliant
feathered headdress. THEY help
MOCTEZUMA into the regal attire and
worship HIM. ALL freeze as lights
change and MALINALLI appears.)

MALINALLI
(to Audience)
AND SO THE BOY THE AZTECS THOUGHT THEY KNEW
BECAME THE KING, WITH GOLDEN SANDALS TOO
THEN, SEVENTEEN YEARS WOULD PASS
AN OCEAN AWAY WHERE HATUEY
MADE HIS STAND AND DIED…
FATE FOUND A MAN
IN SEARCH OF DIFFERENT SKIES...

(ALL exit.)

SETTING: Cuba, 1519. The home of HERNÁN
                                            CORTÉZ.

AT RISE:

                    (HERNÁN CORTÉZ, 30s, sits at a desk
                     composing a letter. Projected
                     behind HIM is the portrait of a
                     well-dressed, beautiful young
                     woman: HIS wife, Catalina.)

4. <u>**SOMEWHERE**</u>

                         CORTÉZ
        I KNOW WHAT NEEDS TO BE SAID
        BUT SOMEHOW, I STILL CAN'T SEEM
        TO WRITE IT DOWN

        WILL YOU UNDERSTAND
        WHY I'M GOING ON THIS EXPEDITION
        OUT ON THE OCEAN AGAIN?

        WHAT WILL YOU SAY
        WHEN YOU FIND THIS NOTE
        UPON THE TABLE?

        WHEN I'M FAR AWAY
        WILL YOU WEEP AND WONDER FOREVER
        IF I REALLY EVER LOVED YOU?

        THIS MAN, CORTÉZ
        THIS MAN THAT YOU THINK
        YOU KNOW SO WELL

        THIS MAN WILL CHANGE
        THAT DAY WHEN YOU READ THIS LETTER
        BUT, CATALINA DON'T FEEL BLAMED

        SOMEWHERE

SOMEWHERE THERE IS SOMETHING
THAT I HAVE TO FIND
SOMETHING THAT I'LL NEVER
FIND HERE BY YOUR SIDE

I DON'T KNOW WHAT IT IS
SO I MUST TAKE THIS CHANCE AND FIND OUT
BUT, IT'S NOT YOUR FAULT

I CAME TO CUBA THINKING IT WAS HERE
DREAMS WERE REAL AND YOU APPEARED
WE BEGAN BUT MY DREAMS STILL
UNFULFILLED BECKONED STILL

EVERY MAN MUST MAKE HIS MARK
I HEAR THE SIREN'S SONG
TODAY I WILL EMBARK TO

SOMEWHERE
SOMEWHERE WHERE THERE IS SOMETHING
I MUST FIND
TO THAT PLACE WHERE ALL MY DREAMS
WILL SPRING TO LIFE

I DON'T KNOW WHERE THAT IS
BUT I WILL TAKE THIS CHANCE AND FIND OUT
I CAN'T BACK DOWN

SOMEWHERE
OUT UPON THE WIND AND OCEAN
I SHALL RIDE
A WHOLE NEW WORLD IS WAITING
FOR ME TO ARRIVE
                        (signing the letter)
SINCERELY, HERNÁN
POST SCRIPT: NEVER DOUBT THAT I LOVED YOU
PERHAPS STILL DO...

Somewhere out there, Catalina...

    SOMEWHERE

11

(Lights change. The stage
transforms into the port of Havana
where a Spanish galleon is being
outfitted for its imminent departure.
CREW enters carrying provisions.)

5. <u>CRIMSON TIDE</u>

CREW

OH, OH
OH, OH, OH, OH, OH, OH
OH, OH
OH, OH, OH, OH, OH, OH

LIFE ON THE SEA
IS FULL OF IRONY
WE HOIST HIGH THE SAILS
WE SAY OUR FAREWELLS
BUT IT'S LAND WE WANT TO SEE

WE ARE CONQUISTADORES
WHO PROUDLY REPRESENT SPAIN
WITH A MOUTHFUL OF RUM
WE LOAD ARQUEBUS
AND NO ONE DARES STAND IN OUR WAY

OH, OH
OH, OH, OH, OH, OH, OH
OH, OH
OH, OH, OH, OH, OH, OH

CORTÉZ

OUT ON THE SEA
THERE'S NOWHERE I'D RATHER BE
WITH MY SHIPS AND MY MEN
I'LL SAIL THE HORIZON
IT DOESN'T GET BETTER THAN THIS

(JUAN JARAMILLO, 30s, enters.)

JARAMILLO

THE SUN ON YOUR FACE

                    CORTÉZ
Juan!

                    (THEY shake hands.)

                    JARAMILLO
THE WIND IN YOUR HAIR
TO LOOK UP TO THE SKY
AND SEE STARS EVERYWHERE

                    CORTÉZ
SUCH AN INDESCRIBABLE FEELING

                    CORTÉZ & JARAMILLO
THIS IS WHERE WE WERE MEANT TO BE
WE WERE MEANT FOR LIFE ON THE SEA

                    (The Spanish flag rises upon the
                    masthead.)

                    COMPANY
HOIST HIGH THE SPANISH FLAG
OUR CODE OF ARMS ENSHRINED
LET THE BANNER UNFURL
LET IT SHOW THE WORLD
OUR QUEST IS JUSTIFIED
WE ARE THE CRIMSON TIDE

                    CREW
OH, OH
OH, OH, OH, OH, OH, OH
OH, OH
OH, OH, OH, OH, OH, OH

                    (The loading continues. CORTÉZ and
                    JARAMILLO inspect provisions. DIEGO
                    DE ORDAZ, 50s, and JUAN VELÁSQUEZ
                    DE LEÓN, 30s, enter.)

LEÓN
(to ORDAZ, but looking to
CORTÉZ)
OUT HERE ALL I THINK OF IS HER
AND OF THE DAY I RETURN
OH, UNTIL THAT DAY

LIKE THE DOG HE IS HE LEAVES HER CRYING
CATALINA! IT WAS ME SHE SHOULD HAVE MARRIED
NOW I'M ON THIS SHIP TO PROVE MY LOVE IS
TRUE TO HER

ORDAZ
LEÓN, LET IT GO
CORTÉZ DOESN'T KNOW
THE MAN WHO SENDS HIM
SENDS US FOR CONTROL

WHEN HE GETS OUT OF HAND
HE'S AS GOOD AS DEAD
PUT YOUR RANCOR ASIDE
UNTIL THEN

LET HIM BE FOR A WHILE
UNTIL WE FIND SOME GOLD
THEN CORTÉZ CAN DIE
THEN YOU CAN DEAL YOUR BLOW

(ORDAZ leaves LEÓN to greet
CORTÉZ and JARAMILLO.)

COMPANY
HOIST HIGH THE SPANISH FLAG
OUR CODE OF ARMS ENSHRINED
LET THE BANNER UNFURL
LET IT SHOW THE WORLD
THAT WHAT WE DO IS RIGHT
WE KNOW THE WORLD IS ROUND
WE GO TO MAKE OUR MARK
NEW WORLD: HERE WE COME!

(Lights change and ALL freeze.

14

Spotlight on LEÓN.)

6. JUDGMENT DAY

LEÓN

SHE IS ON MY MIND
MY DREAM EVERY NIGHT
HERE ON THIS GALLEON

AND ONLY GOD KNOWS WHY
I'VE MADE THE ULTIMATE SACRIFICE
COMING HERE

FATHER, CAN YOU HEAR THE SILENCE
EVERY TIME I CALL HER NAME
AND THERE'S NO REPLY?

SINGING OUT THIS LONESOME CHORUS
WHILE THE MELODY PLAYS ON
CAN SHE HEAR ME FROM CUBA?

I'VE COME HERE TO SET HER FREE
TO KILL THE MAN
THAT TOOK HER FROM ME

MY LOVE FOR HER WILL JUSTIFY
LOOKING IN HIS EYES
WHEN I SEND HIM TO HIS GRAVE

AND I KNOW PRAYING FOR FORGIVENESS
WHEN THE DEED THAT I MUST DO
IS HELL SENT

IS JUST LIKE STANDING IN A TEMPEST
YET I WILL STAND STEADFAST AND UNAFRAID
SHE IS WORTH MY JUDGMENT DAY

AND I KNOW
I AM GIVING UP MY SOUL IN THIS ENDEAVOR
MORE THAN GOLD
ARE THE CONTOURS OF HER EYES TO ME

DAMNED I MAY BE
FOLLOWING THIS DREAM
BUT JUST TO HOLD HER IN MY ARMS
THAT'S ALL THE HEAVEN I NEED

YES, I KNOW
I AM GIVING UP MY SOUL IN THIS ENDEAVOR
MORE THAN GOLD ARE HER LIPS, HER EYES, AND
ALL ELSE ABOUT HER TO ME

DAMNED I MAY BE
FOLLOWING THIS DREAM
BUT JUST TO HOLD HER IN MY ARMS
OH, JUST TO HOLD HER IN MY ARMS
YES, JUST TO HOLD HER IN MY ARMS
THAT'S ALL THE HEAVEN I NEED

     (Lights change again, with the
      sounds of hurricane winds, waves
      crashing, thunder cracking. The
      bodies onstage sway in place and
      endure the storm until it subsides.
      MALINALLI appears suddenly, bound
      at the wrists and agitated, slowly
      making HER way to LEÓN.)

            MALINALLI
        (over music, intensely to
         Audience)

Champotón, on the coast of Campeche, year One Rabbit. In the
year of your lord Fifteen-hundred and eighteen. The first to
arrive was Juan de Grijalva with three-hundred men. They filled
me with their merciful god each night, I took their Spanish,
and they returned to the sea as quickly as they came.

That is how Cortéz found me in the Year One Reed. A
worthless slave. A wretched whore. A gift to grizzled
gods. Of no consequence to them but for the temple between
my legs. Until one of them heard me speak!

     (SHE reaches LEÓN as a slave
      in frightful submission. HE takes

hold of the rope around her wrists.
Lights change as the stage transforms
into the sunsoaked beaches of
Veracruz, Mexico in 1519. The
Spaniards draw THEIR swords. An
older TEUHTLILTZIN enters with
TOTONACS behind HIM, all of THEM
carrying gold and jewels destined
for Aztec coffers. The two worlds
meet centerstage.)

7. VERACRUZ, 1519

                    TEUHTLILTZIN
                  (to CORTÉZ)
WELCOME TO OUR LAND
IT'S GOOD TO SEE YOUR KIND AGAIN
YOU ARE THE PART OF THE
PUZZLE I WAS MISSING

WITH YOU IN MY CORNER
I KNOW THAT I CAN HAVE
EVERYTHING THAT
I HAVE EVER DREAMED

                    TOTONACS
                  (pointing to CREW)
THEY ARE GODS AND WE SHOULD BE KNEELING!

                    CORTÉZ
                  (to JARAMILLO)
JUAN, PRAY, WHAT ARE THEY SAYING?

                    TEUHTLILTZIN
                  (to TOTONACS)
LAY THESE GIFTS OF GOLD BEFORE THEM!

                    JARAMILLO
CAPITÁN, THEY'RE NOT SPEAKING MAYAN!

                    ALL
WHAT ARE THEY SAYING?

17

                    (TOTONACS lay the riches at
                    CORTÉZ's feet.)

                            TOTONACS
        WHAT HAVE YOU BROUGHT US?
        WHAT WILL YOU TEACH US?
        HAVE YOU COME TO FREE US?

        WHAT HAVE YOU BROUGHT US?
        WHAT WILL YOU TEACH US?
        HAVE YOU COME TO FREE US?

        WE WORK ALL DAY
        BUT HIDE AT NIGHT
        THAT'S WHEN THEY COME
        FOR VICTIMS TO SACRIFICE

        LIFE IS HARD
        WHEN YOU'RE A SLAVE
        TEULE, HELP
        WE PRAY

        WHAT HAVE YOU BROUGHT US?
        WHAT WILL YOU TEACH US?
        HAVE YOU COME TO FREE US?

        WHAT HAVE YOU BROUGHT US?
        WHAT WILL YOU TEACH US?
        HAVE YOU COME TO FREE US?

                          TEUHTLILTZIN
                          (to CORTÉZ)
        THESE SLAVES ARE JUST A LITTLE
        OVERWHELMED BY YOUR PRESENCE
        FORGIVE THEM IF FOR A MOMENT
        THEY TICKLE YOUR SENSES

            TOTONACS   TEUHTLILTZIN
    WHAT HAVE YOU BROUGHT US?   Quiet, you fools! Silence!
    WHAT WILL YOU TEACH US?   They are the answer to my
    HAVE YOU COME TO FREE US?   prayers, not yours! Silence,
                                   I say! Or I will take you all

WHAT HAVE YOU BROUGHT US?   for the sacrifice!
WHAT WILL YOU TEACH US?
HAVE YOU COME TO FREE US?

        (Pause. Mesmerized by the riches,
         ORDAZ can't help but break in.)

               ORDAZ
            (to CORTÉZ)
REMEMBER TABASCO WHERE THE
CACIQUE GAVE US SLAVE GIRLS?
HE SAID, "THESE ARE ALL YOURS!"
SO WE BROUGHT THEM ON BOARD?

THERE'S SOMETHING I KNOW
I THINK I SHOULD TELL YOU
WE MAY HAVE A TRANSLATOR
I THINK WE COULD USE

              CORTÉZ
What?

             JARAMILLO
            (to ORDAZ)
HOW LONG WERE YOU PLANNING
TO KEEP THIS A SECRET?

You conniving sneak!

              CORTÉZ
Juan!

              ORDAZ
LEÓN, BRING FORTH THE GIRL!

        (LEÓN shoves MALINALLI towards
         ORDAZ.)

              ORDAZ
          (to MALINALLI)
IT'S TIME TO
RENDER YOUR SERVICES

```
    TELL US ALL HE'S SAID
    'CAUSE WE DON'T HAVE A CLUE

    DID HE SAY THAT THIS
    GOLD COMES FROM SOMEWHERE?
    ASK HOW WE GET THERE
    SOMEONE WRITE THIS DOWN!

    LOOK AT HER
    ISN'T SHE PRETTY?
                (pointing to HER breasts)
    LOOK AT THESE!

Anda, preciosa.
La volta!

                (CREW laughs, taunts MALINALLI
                  until SHE falls at CORTÉZ's feet.)

                            CORTÉZ
                        (sternly to CREW)
    LET HER BE
    OR I'LL STRIKE YOU DEAD!
    SHE'S OUR LINK TO THESE PEOPLE
    YET WE TREAT HER THIS WAY
                        (helping MALINALLI stand,
                          over music)
Are you all right?


                        MALINALLI
Yes.

                        CORTÉZ
You speak our language? How?

                        MALINALLI
Your kind has been here before.

                        CORTÉZ
What is your name?

                        MALINALLI
Malinalli.
```

CORTÉZ

Marina...

> (Pause. HE cuts the rope around HER
> wrists, sheathes HIS sword. The
> other Spaniards do the same. SHE
> spots the rosary around HIS neck.
> Mesmerized by it, SHE reaches for
> it, then pulls HER hand back. HE
> removes the rosary and gifts it to
> HER.)

8. <u>DO IT FOR YOUR CREW</u>

ORDAZ
(interrupting)
CAPITÁN, IF YOU'RE THROUGH
WITH YOUR PITY, LEND HER TO ME
WITH ALL THIS GOLD BEFORE US
DON'T YOU SEE THE POSSIBILITIES?

WE WERE SENT OUT HERE
FOR MERE EXPLORATION
BUT SINCE THERE'S GOLD
LET'S TAKE SOME OF IT TOO

CAPITÁN
DO IT FOR YOUR CREW
CAPITÁN

WE'VE FOLLOWED YOU THROUGH WIND AND RAIN
AND NEVER HAVE COMPLAINED
WE'VE RAISED THE MASTS AND SWABBED THE DECKS
ALL DAY AND THEN AGAIN AND AGAIN

WE ASK FOR RESTITUTION NOW
FOR ALL OUR PAIN AND SWEAT
ALL IT TAKES IS JUST A LITTLE GOLD
AND ALL OUR PAIN WE WILL FORGET

                    ORDAZ & CREW
        CAPITÁN
        DO IT FOR YOUR CREW
        CAPITÁN

                      JARAMILLO
                (in protest, to CORTÉZ)
This is mutiny, Hernán! The Gobernador sent us to explore.
These cutthroats want more.

                      CORTÉZ
Stay a moment, Juan.
                    (picking up riches)
They shine ever so brightly, do they not?

                      JARAMILLO

Hernán!

                    ORDAZ & CREW

        CAPTAIN, CAPTAIN
        LISTEN TO US

        CAPTAIN, CAPTAIN
        DO IT FOR US

        CAPTAIN, CAPTAIN
        LISTEN TO US
        GIVE US GOLD
        AND WE'LL SHUT UP

                      CORTÉZ
        WE WERE SENT TO SCOPE THINGS OUT
        BUT ALL THIS GOLD TURNS MY HEAD AROUND
        SUDDENLY I WANT IT ALL!

                    ORDAZ & CREW
        WE WANT GOLD!!!

                      CORTÉZ
        GOLD IS WHAT I'M THINKING OF
                      (to MALINALLI)
        TELL HIM WHAT I SAY
        MARINA, DON'T BE AFRAID

AND TELL ME ALL HE SAYS
DON'T BE AFRAID

        (HE turns HER towards TEUHTLILTZIN,
        whispers in HER ear what HE wants
        HER to say.)

9. DOES YOUR EMPEROR HAVE GOLD?

              MALINALLI
           (to TEUHTLILTZIN)
THERE'S ONE THING I MUST ASK YOU
THERE'S ONE THING I MUST CONFESS
BY BRINGING US THESE GIFTS OF GOLD
I REST ASSURED YOU'VE PASSED THE TEST

YOU SEE, WE'VE TRAVELED FROM ACROSS THE SEA
WE'VE DONE IT TO SAVE YOUR SOULS
WE'RE HERE TO TELL YOU THAT THERE'S JUST ONE GOD
BUT FIRST ONE THING I NEED TO KNOW

DOES YOUR EMPEROR HAVE GOLD?
DOES YOUR EMPEROR HAVE GOLD?
DO YOU WANT TO SAVE YOUR SOULS?
DOES YOUR EMPEROR HAVE GOLD?

WE'VE HEARD ABOUT YOUR CITY
WHERE STREETS ARE PAVED WITH GOLD
NOW TELL US: IS IT A LEGEND?
OR ARE THERE TREASURES UNTOLD?

DOES YOUR EMPEROR HAVE GOLD?
DOES YOUR EMPEROR HAVE GOLD?
IF YOU WANT TO SAVE YOUR SOULS

             ORDAZ & CREW
YOUR EMPEROR BETTER HAVE GOLD!

        MALINALLI, CORTÉZ, ORDAZ & CREW
YOU SEE WE HAVE A DISEASE
THAT ONLY GOLD CAN APPEASE
AND WE'RE DYING TO FIND THE CURE

DOES YOUR EMPEROR HAVE GOLD?
DOES YOUR EMPEROR HAVE GOLD?

                         TEUHTLILTZIN
IF YOU WANT AN ANSWER
THEN YOU NEED NOT ASK AGAIN
THE EMPEROR'S HALLS ARE FILLED WITH GOLD
THERE ABIDES THE CURE FOR YOUR PAIN

NOW AS A TOKEN OF PEACE
I ASK FOR JUST ONE THING
THE HEADDRESS ON YOUR HEAD
I ASK YOU FOR MY KING

                    TEUHTLILTZIN, CREW, & TOTONACS
MY/HIS/OUR EMPEROR HAS GOLD
MY/HIS/OUR EMPEROR HAS GOLD
MY/HIS/OUR EMPEROR HAS GOLD
MY/HIS/OUR EMPEROR HAS GOLD

        (CORTÉZ hesitates, but eventually
         removes HIS helmet and gives it to
         MALINALLI. SHE hands it to
         TEUHTLILTZIN. HE scuttles away with
         TOTONACS behind HIM.)

        (The CREW congratulate ORDAZ and
         CORTÉZ as THEY inspect the riches.
         THEY all freeze when the lights
         change. Spotlight on MALINALLI
         looking straight at CORTÉZ.)

10. <u>HERNÁN CORTÉZ</u>

                         MALINALLI
HE ASKED ME WHAT ELSE I HEARD TODAY
BUT WHAT I HEARD WORDS COULDN'T SAY
WHEN HE WAS STANDING RIGHT THERE

I FELT THE EARTH SHAKE AND IN MY HEART
A SUBTLE MELODY PLAYED ON
SO, I LOOKED AT HIM AND STARED

I'VE NEVER DREAMED OF BEING ANYTHING
OTHER THAN THE SLAVE HE SEES
YET IN HIS EYES I SEE A DIFFERENT ME

I MUST BE WRONG FOR NOW IT SEEMS
THIS WORLD HAS MORE TO OFFER ME
IS THIS SOME CRAZY DREAM?

OH, GODS ABOVE, ENLIGHTEN ME
GIVE ME SOME SIGN THAT WILL SHOW ME
WHAT ALL THIS REALLY MEANS?
WHAT IS THIS STRANGE NEW SENSATION
I HAVE NEVER FELT BEFORE?
THIS MUSIC PLAYING IN MY SOUL

HERNÁN CORTÉZ
HE'S IN MY HEAD
I GET THIS FEELING JUST TO HEAR HIS NAME
THEN SUDDENLY I SWEAR
I SEE HIM STANDING THERE
SMILING AT ME

HERNÁN CORTÉZ
MAKES ME FORGET
THE WRONG THAT THIS CRUEL WORLD HAS DONE TO ME
AND LONELINESS TURNS TO SOMETHING ELSE INSTEAD
WHEN I THINK ABOUT HERNÁN CORTÉZ

I STILL HAVEN'T FORGOTTEN
WHAT THE AZTECS DID TO ME
AN ORPHANED CHILD WITH NOBLE BLOOD
BECAME A DISTANT DREAM

AND I BECAME A SLAVE
WHEN I SHOULD HAVE BEEN MALINTZIN
THIS MAN MAY BE MY ONLY CHANCE
TO RESURRECT THAT OLD SCENE

HE WILL BE MY INSPIRATION
AND I WILL BE HIS FORM OF SPEECH
UNTIL HE LOVES ME

HE WILL LOVE ME

HERNÁN CORTÉZ
HE'S IN MY HEAD
I GET THIS FEELING JUST TO HEAR HIS NAME
THEN SUDDENLY I SWEAR
I SEE HIM STANDING THERE SMILING AT ME

HERNÁN CORTÉZ
MAKES ME FORGET
THE WRONG THAT THIS CRUEL WORLD HAS DONE TO ME
AND LONELINESS TURNS TO SOMETHING ELSE INSTEAD
WHEN I THINK ABOUT HERNÁN CORTÉZ
WHEN I DREAM ABOUT HERNÁN CORTÉZ
WHEN I THINK ABOUT HERNÁN CORTÉZ

    (Blackout.)

SETTING: MOCTEZUMA's Palace in
                                      Tenochtitlán.

AT RISE:

                    (An older, tense MOCTEZUMA sits on
                     HIS throne, holding CORTÉZ's
                     helmet. Projected onto the
                     background is the image of the
                     Aztec god Quetzalcoatl, who bears a
                     striking resemblance to CORTÉZ.)

11. <u>WHAT WILL HAPPEN TO US?</u>

                              MOCTEZUMA
IF I SAT DOWN AND CRIED
COULD I OPEN MY EYES
AND SEE THAT THIS THREAT
IS GONE?

IF I PRAYED TO THE GODS
WISHED ON EVERY STAR
COULD I WAKE UP AND FIND
I'M DREAMING?

NOW I'M FACED WITH DECIDING
THE FATE OF A SOCIETY
THAT HAS PLACED ME
WHERE I STAND

WILL I BE TO BLAME
IF FATE HAS ITS WAY
AND I WELCOME THEM
INTO OUR LAND?

WHY DID YOU HAVE TO COME DURING MY REIGN?
WHY COULDN'T YOU JUST WAIT AND COME SOME
OTHER DAY?
I'VE COME TO LOVE
TENOCHTITLÁN

YOU WERE JUST A TALE UNTIL TODAY
BUT NOW YOU STAND UPON THE SHORE
WAITING TO TAKE BACK WHAT'S YOURS
CAN THIS BE SO?

WHAT WILL HAPPEN TO US
IF IT ALL GOES YOUR WAY?
CAN'T YOU TAKE WHAT YOU WANT
WHEN WERE BURIED AND DEAD?

WHAT WILL HAPPEN TO US?
QUETZALCOATL, I PRAY
WHAT WILL HAPPEN TO US
WHEN YOU TAKE WHAT WE'VE WORKED FOR AWAY?
WHEN YOU TAKE WHAT YOU'VE GIVEN AWAY?

I HAVE DONE MY BEST TO SERVE YOU
RAISED COUNTLESS TEMPLES IN YOUR NAME
AXAYACATL WAS MY FATHER
AND HE TAUGHT ME HOW TO PRAY
TO YOU

ALL YOU'VE ASKED I'VE ALWAYS DONE
I HAVE BEEN YOUR FAITHFUL SON
EVEN WHEN YOU'VE ASKED ME FOR BLOOD
I'VE GIVEN IT TO YOU
I'VE GIVEN IT TO YOU

WHAT WILL HAPPEN TO US
IF IT ALL GOES YOUR WAY?
CAN'T YOU TAKE WHAT YOU WANT
WHEN WE'RE BURIED AND DEAD?

WHAT WILL HAPPEN TO US?
OH, TEULE, I PRAY
WHAT WILL HAPPEN TO US
WHEN YOU TAKE WHAT WE'VE WORKED FOR AWAY
WHEN YOU TAKE WHAT YOU'VE GIVEN AWAY
WILL YOU TAKE ALL THAT WE HAVE AWAY?
                    (uneasy, calling offstage)

Cuauhtémoc!

                    (A flustered TECUICHPO, late teens,
                     enters.)

                         TECUICHPO
Father, a word, please.

                         MOCTEZUMA
Not now, Daughter. I await Cuauhtémoc.

                         TECUICHPO
He is the reason I am here. Tahtli, I do not love him.

                         MOCTEZUMA
                         (rising)
That again!

                         TECUICHPO
Tahtli, please!

                         MOCTEZUMA
Enough! You will marry Cuauhtémoc. Just as your mother
married me. Just as tradition commands it!

                    (TECUICHPO hangs HER head. Catching
                     HIMSELF, HE approaches HER gently,
                     places a hand on HER shoulder, just
                     as a father would.)

                         MOCTEZUMA
                    (staring at helmet)
The world turns faster than ever now, Tecuichpo. At her
deathbed, I promised your mother to do everything in my
power to keep you from falling off. Do not forget that.
                    (shouting offstage again)
Cuauhtémoc!

                    (HE hurries off. Alone now,
                     TECUICHPO contemplates HER plight.)

12. __ZENZONTLE__

TECUICHPO

I REMEMBER AS A CHILD-I REMEMBER IT SO WELL
THAT BEAUTIFUL STORY MOTHER USED TO TELL
"WHEN YOU HEAR ZENZONTLE SING
CHILD, IT MEANS THAT LIFE WILL SOON BEGIN

"YES, HE SINGS ALL THE TIME BUT SOMEHOW YOU WILL KNOW
WHEN THE SONG HE SINGS IS MEANT FOR YOU
THE MOST WONDERFUL MELODY INSIDE
LEAVES YOUR HEART NO PLACE TO HIDE"

ZENZONTLE, SING ALL MY DOUBTS AWAY
I YEARN FOR THE MELODY OF LIFE'S EMBRACE
BRING BIG DREAMS ON YOUR WINGS MY WAY
MY HEART YEARNS TO DANCE TO THE SONG YOU PLAY
SOMETHING SUBLIME
OR SUNG HIGH
ANY SOUND WILL DO
ANY SOUND IS FINE

MOCKINGBIRD, NOW THAT I'M SEVENTEEN
PERCH ON MY SHOULDER-WHISPER SOFTLY
SING A SWEET SONG THAT MAKES ME BELIEVE
THERE'S SO MUCH OUT THERE WAITING FOR ME
THEN UNCLIP MY WINGS
TAKE ME SOARING THROUGH THE WIND

TELL ME MY FATHER WILL UNDERSTAND
I AM A PRINCESS WITH MY OWN PLANS
HOW CAN I DO THIS THING HE DEMANDS
MARRY CUAUHTÉMOC-GIVE HIM MY HAND
WHEN I'M SO FAR FROM LOVE
ZENZONTLE FLY TO ME
WITH THAT SONG OF SONGS
THAT I'VE BEEN DREAMING OF

ZENZONTLE, SING ALL MY DOUBTS AWAY
I YEARN FOR THE MELODY OF LIFE'S EMBRACE
BRING BIG DREAMS ON YOUR WINGS MY WAY

MY HEART WANTS TO DANCE TO THE SONG YOU PLAY
SOMETHING SUBLIME
OR SUNG HIGH
ANY SOUND WILL DO
ANY SOUND IS FINE

       (CUAUHTÉMOC, 20s, enters. HE's been
       listening in secret.)

             TECUICHPO
Cuauhtémoc? How long have you been listening?

             CUAUHTÉMOC
Long enough, Cousin.

             TECUICHPO
Father is searching for you. Please, go. I wish to be
alone now.

13. <u>YOU WILL LOVE ME</u>

             CUAUHTÉMOC
THERE IS NO OTHER WAY
TO SAY WHAT I MUST SAY TO YOU
BUT I KNOW YOU SHOULD LOVE ME

NOW THIS THING WE BOTH MUST DO
THAT THROUGH OUR LOVE WE SHOULD ENDURE
WILL SHOW YOU YOU SHOULD LOVE ME

OH, TECUICHPO, IT'S A CRUEL WORLD
RIPE FOR WOMEN NOT FOR LITTLE GIRLS
I'M THE MAN TO SHOW YOU ALL YOU CAN BE WORTH
TRUST IN ME, AND YOU WILL SEE…

             TECUICHPO
             (pulling away)
No, Cousin. I can't. You and Father, you just don't
understand. There is something out there, something just
for me, and I feel, I know…

                         CUAUHTÉMOC
                      (growing impatient)
Tell me, Tecuichpo. What is it you know and feel?

                         TECUICHPO
That something...is not you.

                         CUAUHTÉMOC
                      (unaffected, coming close
                      again)
        THERE IS NO OTHER WAY
        TO SAY WHAT I MUST SAY TO YOU
        BUT KNOW THIS…
        BUT KNOW THIS…

                 (HE attempts a kiss, but SHE
                  resists. HE takes hold of HER
                  forcefully.)

                         CUAUHTÉMOC
        YOU WILL LOVE ME!!!

                 (HE takes HIS kiss, looks upon a
                  disgusted, confused TECUICHPO. SHE
                  dashes off and HE follows.)

                 (Lights change. MALINALLI and
                  CORTÉZ appear. CORTÉZ sleeps while
                  MALINALLI sits nearby, studying the
                  rosary HE gave HER. TEUHTLILTZIN
                  enters secretly, carrying CORTÉZ's
                  helmet.)

14. THE DEAL

                         TEUHTLILTZIN
        HE COULD NOT HAVE COME
        AT A BETTER TIME
        EVERY ACE IN THE DECK
        I DEAL IS MINE

```
                        THEY ARE FEW,
                        THAT IS TRUE
                        BUT WITH THIS LIE
                        I AM SURE WE CAN DO IT IF WE TRY


                                    MALINALLI
                              (rising, over music)
          How did you get in here?


                                    TEUHTLILTZIN
          The same as you, Malinche.


                                    MALINALLI
          Malinche?


                                    TEUHTLILTZIN
          Yes. It is you I have come to see. Not him.


                                    MALINALLI
          Why me?


                                    TEUHTLILTZIN
                        THE CAPITÁN, HE HAS COME
                        ON THIS GLORIOUS OCCASION
                        TO LEAD US, AS HE SAYS,
                        AWAY FROM OUR DAMNATION

                        BUT WHAT IF I COULD PROMISE
                        ALL THE GOLD HE WANTS?
                        AND ALL HE'D HAVE TO DO
                        WOULD BE TO PLAY THE GAME LIKE THIS:


                                    MALINALLI
          What game?


                                    TEUHTLILTZIN
                        MARCH INTO THE CAPITAL
                        AND STAND BEFORE MY KING
                        PROCLAIM HE IS THE TRUE GOD,
                        QUETZALCOATL, COME AGAIN
                        THAT'S ALL HE HAS TO DO
                        I'LL TAKE CARE OF THE REST
```

33

```
                                ALL THE GOLD HE WANTS
                                IF HE CAN PASS THE TEST
                                IMPRESS...
                                AND GIVE TO THEM THE GOD CORTÉZ...


                                        MALINALLI
                    The god Cortéz? But, how? Why?


                                        TEUHTLILTZIN
                                THERE'S SOMETHING I WANT
                                SWEET CHILD, LET ME TELL YOU
                                I WANT TO BE EMPEROR
                                NO LESS AND NO MORE

                                A SMALL PRICE TO PAY
                                FOR FUTURE ENDEAVORS
                                I MAKE ALL THE GOLD HIS
                                HE GIVES ME MY SCORE

                                THINK OF IT, MALINCHE
                                WITH ME IN THE TOP SEAT
                                EVERY LAST TITHING
                                WE'D SPLIT INTO TWO

                                YEAR AFTER YEAR
                                HE'D SET SAIL WITH GOLD IN TOW
                                TAKE ALL THE PROFITS HOME
                                THEN COME BACK FOR MORE
```

TEUHTLILTZIN	MALINALLI
THAT'S ALL	Your people killed my father,
NO LESS AND NO MORE	my brothers! You made me a
YEAR AFTER YEAR	slave! There's nothing I want
HE'LL COME BACK FOR MORE	from you! Ever!

```
                                TEUHTLILTZIN
                                SIDE BY SIDE
                                YOU AND HIM THEY'LL REVERE


                            (HE offers HER the helmet.)
```

                    MALINALLI

What?

                    TEUHTLILTZIN

A god, Malinche. That's what he will be. With you, right by
his side. Your past? All of it will be forgotten, while
everyone adores you. But only you can help him do this.

                    MALINALLI

Me?

                    TEUHTLILTZIN

No one else. Only you, Malinche.

               (Glimpsing all of the
                possibilities, SHE finally takes
                the helmet.)

                    MALINALLI

Only me. But what must I do?

                    TEUHTLILTZIN

Clever girl!

        ON THE SOLSTICE
        BID HIM WEAR THIS
        REACH THE CAUSEWAY
        TO OUR LAND

        GIVE THE AZTECS
        THEIR PLUMED SERPENT
        THEN UNFURL HIS
        CRIMSON FLAGS

        AND AS OUR SPEARS
        LIE SILENT
        MARCH INTO
        TENOCHTITLÁN

        THE AGE OF MALINCHE
        WILL DAWN ON THAT DAY
        WE'LL WRITE OUR OWN CODEX
        INCLUDE BOTH OUR NAMES

```
          POPOCATÉPETL HERSELF
          WE'LL AMAZE
          WHEN CEM ANÁHUAC
          LEARNS TO DO THINGS OUR WAY

          MOCTEZUMA
          TIME TO MAKE IT MINE, ALL MINE
          XOCOYOTZIN
          WATCH TEUHTLILTZIN RISE!
```

> (TEUHTLILTZIN scurries off. CORTÉZ
> wakes with a start. MALINALLI hides
> the helmet behind HER.)

                    CORTÉZ

What?!

                    MALINALLI

It's only me, Hernán. No one else.
                    (backing off to exit)
I'll fetch your meal.

                    CORTÉZ

Wait. Not yet. Come, sit with me.

                    MALINALLI

As you wish.

> (SHE sits down. HE wraps an arm
> around HER, pulls HER close.)

                    CORTÉZ

I was dreaming. A city of gold, and you and I were in it.

                    MALINALLI

You and I?

                    CORTÉZ

Yes.

                              MALINALLI

And your men?

                              CORTÉZ

I don't recall seeing them. The irony...

                              MALINALLI

What?

                              CORTÉZ

The one place they yearn to find evades them, even in my dreams.

                              MALINALLI

Why, do you think?

                              CORTÉZ

Because I don't know how to get there without risking all
of our lives.
                         (beat, sensually caressing
                          HER face)
Finding you, I thought you could help me find all the
answers. I still believe that. Do you, Marina?

                              MALINALLI

Hernán, I...

15. <u>ALL YOU NEED TO DO</u>

                              CORTÉZ
           HERE WE ARE AGAIN, YOU AND I, FACE TO FACE
           WHILE THE WORLD OUTSIDE SLOWLY TURNS
           I SEE YOU SMILE
           AND THAT'S ALL YOU NEED TO DO

           THEN SOMEWHERE IS HERE HOLDING ON
           YOU ARE ALL I'M SURE OF

           SO MUCH YOU COULD SAY
           TO QUELL THESE DOUBTS INSIDE MY HEAD
           BUT I SEE YOU SMILE AND
           THAT'S ALL YOU NEED TO DO

                    (THEY embrace.)

                         37

                    MALINALLI
IN YOUR WARM EMBRACE I CAN FEEL EVERY
BREATH YOU TAKE
WHILE THE WORLD OUTSIDE WAITS FOR YOU
I'M IN YOUR ARMS AND
THAT'S ALL YOU NEED TO DO

TO MAKE ME BELIEVE IN THIS LOVE
WHILE THE GODS BLESS US FROM ABOVE

SO MUCH WE COULD SAY
BEFORE THIS WORLD SWEEPS US AWAY
BUT I'M IN YOUR ARMS AND
THAT'S ALL YOU NEED TO DO

                    CORTÉZ
YOU HAVE COME MY WAY

                    MALINALLI
YOU HAVE COME MY WAY

                CORTÉZ & MALINALLI
AND I WILL NEVER LET YOU GO

                    MALINALLI
LOVE IS HERE TO STAY?

                    CORTÉZ
I PROMISE YOU THAT COME WHAT MAY

                CORTÉZ & MALINALLI
YOU'RE IN MY HEART
YOU'RE IN MY SOUL
AND TOGETHER WE WILL GO
WHERE THE PYRAMIDS BLEED GOLD AND JADE…

                    CORTÉZ
HERE WE ARE AGAIN, YOU AND I…

                    MALINALLI
YOU AND I?

                    CORTÉZ & MALINALLI
LET THE WORLD OUTSIDE CRASH AND BURN

                    CORTÉZ
I SEE YOU SMILE…

                    MALINALLI
I SEE YOU SMILE…

                    CORTÉZ & MALINALLI
I SEE YOU SMILE AND
THAT'S ALL YOU NEED TO DO

YOU'RE IN MY ARMS AND
THAT'S ALL YOU NEED TO DO

                (THEY kiss. SHE remembers the
                 helmet and quickly rises.)

                    MALINALLI
Hernán, I have something to tell you.

                    CORTÉZ
Yes? What is it?

                (THEY freeze. Lights change as
                 TEUHTLILTZIN, MOCTEZUMA, and
                 CUAUHTÉMOC enter.)

16. <u>**THE DEAL (REPRISE)**</u>

                    TEUHTLILTZIN
                  (to MOCTEZUMA)
TLATOANI, I RETURN
ON THIS GLORIOUS OCCASION
TOWING GREENSTONE AND GOLD
FROM OUR TRIBUTARY NATIONS

AND MY THE THINGS I'VE SEEN
OH, YOU JUST WON'T BELIEVE
BEARDED LONG-LOST GODS
ONE HOPED YOU ENJOYED

```
                    HIS HEADDRESS
                    THE GREAT QUETZALCOATL CORTÉZ

                    THERE'S SOMETHING I KNOW
                    SIT DOWN, LET ME TELL YOU
                    THE EAGLE HAS LANDED
                    BUT HE'S GOT PLANS TO SOAR

                    HE GLADLY ACCEPTED
                    MY KIND INVITATION
                    TO PICK OUT HIS TEMPLE
                    PERCHED ON THE SUN STONE
```

                              CUAUHTÉMOC

What?!

                              MOCTEZUMA
                           (prophetically)

He comes...

                              CUAUHTÉMOC
                         (threatening, to
                           TEUHTLILTZIN)
```
            LOST GODS AND WILD TALES
            I SEE PAST YOUR SLEEKNESS
```

You deceitful snake!

                              MOCTEZUMA

Cuauhtémoc!

                              TEUHTLILTZIN
```
            NO!
            HEAR THE JAGUAR THAT ROARS!
```

```
       TEUHTLILTZIN                    CUAUHTÉMOC
    THAT'S ALL                 WHAT WILL HAPPEN TO US
    NO NEED TO WANT MORE       IF THESE GODS COME TO STAY?
    GODS REWARD CHILDREN       WILL THEY TAKE WHAT THEY
    THAT DO AS THEY'RE TOLD    WANT?
                               GIVE TEUHTLILTZIN HIS WAY?
```

                    TEUHTLILTZIN & CUAUHTÉMOC
    JAGUARS SMILE
    GOING IN FOR THE KILL!

                            MOCTEZUMA
Enough!!!
                        (beat)
Speak, Teuhtliltzin. Tell me what I must do?

                          TEUHTLILTZIN
Of course.

                (Lights up on MALINALLI and CORTÉZ
                 again as SHE finally reveals the
                 helmet.)

                            CORTÉZ
                      (rising, angry)
Then he was here? How, and when? Why didn't you wake me?
What did he say to you?

        TEUHTLILTZIN   MALINALLI
    (to MOCTEZUMA)   (to CORTÉZ, giving HIM helmet)
    AT THE SOLSTICE   On the solstice
    YOU MUST GREET HIM   you must wear this,
    ON THE CAUSEWAY   on the causeway...
    TO OUR LAND

                          CUAUHTÉMOC
Uncle, no!

        TEUHTLILTZIN   MALINALLI
    THEN REGALE HIM   Be their plumed serpent,
    OUR PLUMED SERPENT   Hernán.
    AND REVERE HIS   Show them your mighty power!
    CRIMSON FLAGS

                          CUAUHTÉMOC
He betrays us!

                              41

TEUHTLILTZIN	MALINALLI
AND WITH OUR SPEARS	Then, together, you and I, we
LYING SILENT	will march into Tenochtitlán,
GIVE HIM ALL	yes?
TENOCHTITLÁN	You and I, Hernán, yes?

(CORTÉZ regards the helmet in HIS
hands.)

CUAUHTÉMOC

Tetlatzin, listen!

TEUHTLILTZIN

THE AGE OF TEUHTLILTZIN
WILL DAWN ON THAT DAY
I'LL WRITE MY OWN CODEX
IN BLOOD SIGN MY NAME

AND IZACCÍHUATL
HERSELF I'LL AMAZE
WHEN CEM ANÁHUAC
LEARNS THAT GODS COME TO STAY

MOCTEZUMA
TIME TO MAKE IT MINE, ALL MINE
XOCOYOTZIN
SEE THIS JAGUAR RISE!

(Lights change as LEÓN and ORDAZ
enter.)

17. <u>PROMISES</u>

ORDAZ
(to LEÓN)
MY FRIEND, I KNOW WHAT YOU YEARN TO DO
I SEE THE VENGEANCE IN YOUR EYES
I FOREVER WILL STAND BY YOUR SIDE
BUT WE MUST BIDE OUR TIME

I KNOW THAT HE STOLE YOUR LOVE

BUT REMEMBER WHAT WE CAME FOR
WAIT UNTIL WE FIND MORE GOLD
THEN YOU CAN DEAL YOUR BLOW

                    LEÓN

DON'T YOU UNDERSTAND
SHE'S ALL I'VE EVER DREAMED
SHE IS THE REASON
I HAVE CROSSED THE SEA
CATALINA SHOULD HAVE MARRIED ME
FOR THAT CORTÉZ MUST BLEED

                    ORDAZ

ALL I'M ASKING IS FOR SOME TIME
WE WILL BOTH MAKE SURE HE DIES
BUT NOT YET-WHEN THE TIME IS RIGHT
WILL YOU CHANGE YOUR MIND?

          (JARAMILLO enters.)

                 JARAMILLO
               (in protest, to CORTÉZ)
  HERNÁN, DO YOU REALIZE WHAT THIS MEANS?
  THIS CHANGES EVERYTHING WE CAME HERE FOR
  IS THIS TREASON WORTH ITS WEIGHT IN GOLD?

            CORTÉZ   JARAMILLO
SEE THE POSSIBILITIES OF WHAT   OH, NO, NO, NO
I HAVE IN MIND
WE HAVE THE CHANCE OF A   NO, HERNÁN, NO!
LIFETIME HERE
MY MISSION NOW IS ALL TOO
CLEAR
Can I count on you, Juan?

                 JARAMILLO
I don't know. I just don't know...

                 CORTÉZ
  EVERY MAN MUST MAKE HIS MARK
  MAKE HIS STAND OR WHEN HE IS GONE
  NO ONE GIVES A DAMN WHO HE WAS

                    43

MY TIME IS NOW—MY TIME HAS COME

IN EVERY MAN'S LIFE THERE COMES A DECISION
THE ONE THAT WILL CHANGE IT ALL FOREVER
THIS IS THE MOMENT I MARK UPON HISTORY
MY FRIEND, WILL YOU STAND BY ME?

                         TEUHTLILTZIN
HOW LONG I HAVE WAITED FOR THIS CHANCE
SOON I WILL STAND WHERE HE STANDS
SOON I WILL STAND
WHERE I WAS MEANT TO STAND

MOCTEZUMA
TIME TO MAKE IT MINE, ALL MINE
XOCOYOTZIN
YOU SHALL BE MY SACRIFICE

                         MALINALLI
JUST TO BE
ALL HERNÁN NEEDS
SPEAK THROUGH ME
HE IS ALL I SEE

             (The rest of the Company enters.
              Characters with asterisks below
              sing simultaneously.)

                         MALINALLI*
I WILL AID HIM
I WILL SOOTHE HIM
IN THE DARKNESS
I WILL HOLD HIM

TAKE EACH MOMENT
AS A PROMISE
TO THE LOVE THAT
GROWS WITHIN ME

                         CORTÉZ*
SOMEWHERE
THIS IS THAT PLACE

WHERE THIS FINE GOD WILL LEAD FIVE-HUNDRED MEN
THROUGH THE SWAMPS OF TEXCOCO
AND BY GOD, WE WILL WIN!

                    MOCTEZUMA*

WHAT WILL HAPPEN TO US
WHEN THIS GOD COMES TO US
TO RECLAIM WHAT IS HIS?
SHOULD WE FEAR HIM?

                    TECUICHPO*

CUAUHTÉMOC, I TOLD YOU BEFORE
NO!

                    CUAUHTÉMOC*

TECUICHPO, I'LL TELL YOU ONCE MORE
YES!

                    LEÓN*

CATALINA!

                    ORDAZ*

CAPTAIN, CAPTAIN, LISTEN TO US!
CAPTAIN, CAPTAIN, DO IT FOR US!

                    JARAMILLO*

HERNÁN!

                    AZTECS*

MOCTEZUMA
OH, OH, OH, OH, OH
XOCOYOTZIN
OH, OH, OH, OH, OH, OH, OH

                    CREW*

EL CAUDILLO
OH, OH, OH, OH, OH
EL CAUDILLO
OH, OH, OH, OH, OH, OH, OH

                          COMPANY
IN EVERYONE'S LIFE THERE COMES A DECISION
THE ONE THAT WILL CHANGE IT ALL FOREVER
THIS IS THE MOMENT WE MARK UPON HISTORY

                  CORTÉZ & MOCTEZUMA
               (to respective followers)
WILL YOU STAND BY ME?

          (MALINALLI finally places the helmet on
          CORTÉZ's head. The CREW and AZTECS cheer
          "Santiago!" and "Ayyo!"
          respectively.)

                          COMPANY
PROMISES, PROMISES
SOMETIMES ARE TREACHEROUS
STILL WE MUST GO
OUR OWN WAY

WHEN LIFE IS THE
ULTIMATE PROMISE MADE
YOU LIVE AND DIE
BY WHAT YOU SAY

IN EVERYONE'S LIFE
THERE COMES A DECISION
THE ONE THAT WILL
CHANGE IT ALL FOREVER

THIS IS THE MOMENT
WE MARK UPON HISTORY
YEAR ONE REED!!!

          (Blackout.)

                   END OF ACT I

ACT II

SCENE 1

SETTING: Intersection of Space and Time.

AT RISE:

      (Darkness. Spotlight on MALINALLI,
      again.)

18. **THE STORY YOU WILL KNOW**

              MALINALLI

AND THE SONG PLAYS ON
RINGING IN MY HEAD
ALL THOSE VOICES
THE LIES AND THE CHOICES I MADE
THOSE I BETRAYED
THAT STORY YOU ALREADY KNOW

BUT THAT SONG IS WRONG
I THOUGHT LOVE WAS DEAD
FROM THE SHADOWS
I SUFFERED THE ARROWS AND FLED
FLED, FLED AWAY
AND THAT'S THE STORY YOU WILL KNOW

      (SHE exits. TECUICHPO enters,
      carrying an offering to the gods.)

19. **TECUICHPO'S PRAYER**

              TECUICHPO

I HAVE DREAMS
IN MY LIFE
I HAVE BEEN TOO SCARED TO FOLLOW
BUT I AM OLDER NOW AND
SOMETHING IS TELLING ME
TODAY MAY BE THE START
OF MY TOMORROW

```
I HAVE HOPES
FLYING HIGH
HIGHER THAN THE EAGLES DARE
OVER POPOCATÉPETL AND BEYOND
ACROSS THE OCEAN
ALL MY DREAMS ARE THERE

OH, BUT LOVE IS SOMETHING SPECIAL
WHEN IT'S ALL YOUR DREAMS ARE MADE OF
```

Xochiquetzal, goddess of love and flowers, accept this offering I bring to you. Grant me the fortune to find the love I yearn for-a love filled with all my dreams and desires. And while the prayers on this night are as countless as the citlaltin covering the night sky, promise me my single wish illuminates above all others, because the only one you're listening to is me!

```
BECAUSE LOVE IS SOMETHING SPECIAL
WHEN IT'S ALL YOUR DREAMS ARE MADE OF

NOW I'VE CHOSEN A STAR
OH, THE BRIGHTEST ONE OF ALL
MAKE IT SHINE JUST FOR ME
IN THE SKY

FOREVER BURNING
MY BEACON OF HOPE
AFLAME IN THE HEAVENS
WHERE I KNOW YOU WON'T IGNORE

WHAT I WANT
WHAT I NEED
WHAT IT IS
I'M LIVING FOR

IN THAT LIGHT
YOU WILL SEE
WHO IT IS
I'M MEANT TO BE
```

FOREVER BURNING
MY BEACON OF HOPE
AFLAME IN THE HEAVENS
WHERE I KNOW YOU CAN'T IGNORE
ME...

        (Lights change as stage transforms
        into the causeway leading into
        Tenochtitlán. MOCTEZUMA,
        CUAUHTÉMOC, TEUHTLILTZIN, and
        AZTECS enter, the latter carrying
        gold and jewels. MALINALLI, CORTÉZ
        and rest of the Spaniards enter and
        meet THEM centerstage.)

20. <u>**WELCOME TO TENOCHTITLÁN (REPRISE)**</u>

                         AZTECS & TEUHTLILTZIN
                  (to CORTÉZ)
WELCOME TO TENOCHTITLÁN
TO THE CITY OF THE SUN
THIS IS WHERE THE EAGLE ATE THE SNAKE
THAT IS WHY WE CHOSE TO SETTLE ON THIS LAKE

NO PLACE LIKE TENOCHTITLÁN
CITY UNDERNEATH THE SUN
THE CHAMPION CITY
WHERE EVERYONE WANTS TO BE
TENOCHTITLÁN

                        TEUHTLILTZIN
Hail, Moctezuma! Great emperor of the Mexica! Behold:
QUETZALCOATL CORTÉZ!!!

        (A Spanish cannon booms. The AZTECS
        gasp in awe while mumbles of
        "Quetzalcoatl" can be heard.
        MOCTEZUMA stands frozen.
        TEUHTLILTZIN notices this and
        quickly orders AZTECS to lay the
        gold and jewels at CORTÉZ's feet.)

                    MOCTEZUMA
    I HAVE SAT DOWN AND CRIED
    IN VAIN I HAVE TRIED
    TO THINK THAT THIS THREAT IS GONE

                    MALINALLI
                 (to MOCTEZUMA)
O Great One, my Lord comes as a friend...

                    MOCTEZUMA
    I HAVE PRAYED TO THE GODS
    WISHED ON EVERY STAR
    IN THE HOPE THAT I WAS DREAMING

                    MALINALLI
From across the sea, to witness your great empire...

                    MOCTEZUMA
    NOW I'M FACED WITH DECIDING
    THE FATE OF A SOCIETY
    THAT HAS PLACED ME WHERE I STAND

                    MALINALLI
One thing my Lord desires to know above anything else: Where
may he find more of these precious riches?

                    MOCTEZUMA
    WILL I BE TO BLAME IF FATE HAS ITS WAY
    AND I WELCOME THEM INTO OUR LAND?
    SHOULD I WELCOME THEM INTO OUR LAND?

                    AZTECS & TEUHTLILTZIN
    YES!!!
    GO WELCOME THEM INTO OUR LAND!!!

                (AZTECS shove TECUICHPO toward
                 CORTÉZ. Lights change. CORTÉZ and
                 TECUICHPO lock glances for the
                 first time.)

                    TECUICHPO
I FEEL MY HEART BEATING FASTER...

                    CORTÉZ
IN ALL MY TRAVELS I HAVE NEVER SEEN...

                    TECUICHPO
I FEEL A NEARING DISASTER...

                    CORTÉZ
A GIRL AS BEAUTIFUL AS SHE...

                 TECUICHPO & CORTÉZ
WHY CAN'T I TAKE MY EYES AWAY?
WHY DOES HE/SHE STARE ONLY AT ME?
I GUESS THIS MOMENT IS MEANT TO BE

          (Lights change.)

                    CUAUHTÉMOC
               (tightly, to AZTECS)
ARE THEY EVERYTHING THAT WE DREAMED?

                    AZTECS
WE SEE THE ULTIMATE DEITY!

                    CUAUHTÉMOC
UNSEEN COULD BE THEIR CRUELTY

WHAT WILL HAPPEN TO ALL OF US?
THINK BEFORE YOU SUCCUMB
LONG LOST GODS-IS THAT WHAT YOU YEARN?
                    (to MOCTEZUMA)
UNCLE, YOU MUST DECIDE!

                    AZTECS
YOU CAN'T COMPETE WITH THEM!

                    CUAUHTÉMOC
               (to MOCTEZUMA)
WILL YOU CONCEDE?

Uncle!!!

AZTECS
(to CUAUHTÉMOC)
GUATEMOZÍN-THEY'RE MOVING IN!!!

(AZTECS welcome CORTÉZ and Spaniards
into the city, singing THEM praises,
regaling THEM with even more gold
and jewels.)

AZTECS & TEUHTLILTZIN
WELCOME TO TENOCHTITLÁN
YOUR EVERY WISH IS OUR COMMAND
ENTER YOUR CITY
ALL THAT YOU EVER DREAMED
TENOCHTITLÁN

NO PLACE LIKE TENOCHTITLÁN
COME AND SEE IT NOW FIRSTHAND
TOUR THE CENTRIC
HOME OF THE AZTEC
TENOCHTITLÁN
TENOCHTITLÁN
TENOCHTITLÁN

CUAUHTÉMOC
(sarcastically)
THEY COULD NOT HAVE COME AT A BETTER TIME
LOOK AT HOW YOU GROVEL AT THEIR FEET
THEY ARRIVE, AND YOU JUST CLOSE YOUR EYES
THEN STAY BLIND!
AND WATCH ME AS I CROSS THAT LINE

MOCTEZUMA
Cuauhtémoc-NO!!!

CUAUHTÉMOC
(calculated)
HERNÁN CORTÉZ
TRADITION SAYS
OUR GAME OF TLACHTLI
YOU SHOULD PLAY WITH ME
DISPLAY YOUR DEXTEROUS, WONDROUS,
OMNIPOTENT STRENGTH

52

IMPRESS US, QUETZALCOATL CORTÉZ

> (A hoop, like those used in the
> Mesoamerican game of tlachtli, is
> brought centerstage. CUAUHTÉMOC
> strips down to a loin cloth.)

21. <u>THE BALL GAME/OBSIDIAN BLADE</u>

                    TEUHTLILTZIN
                 (over music)
What is the meaning of this?

                    CORTÉZ
                 (to MALINALLI, confused)
Marina?

                    MALINALLI
                 (concerned)
Tlachtli, Hernán. A difficult game.

                    CORTÉZ

A game?

                    JARAMILLO
Hernán, they outnumber us three-to-one. And on this causeway.
With the lake on both sides. Sound the retreat, now!

                    ORDAZ
                 (cutting in)
Nonsense. Just look at these riches. Do it for your crew,
Capitán, remember?
                 (to CREW)
Yes?

                    CREW
Do it for us, Capitán!

                    CORTÉZ
                 (pushing past THEM)
Get out of my way!

                 (Beat.)

Marina, I play this game, and what happens next?

                    (CREW begins to remove CORTÉZ's
                     armor and urge HIM centerstage.)

                         TEUHTLILTZIN
Cuauhtémoc! You will insult them!

                         CUAUHTÉMOC
Exactly! Out of my way!
                         (to AZTECS)
BALL!!!

                    (A rubber ball is thrown to
                     CUAUHTÉMOC. HE uses HIS forearm to
                     hit the ball and try and get it
                     through the hoop, but misses.
                     AZTECS cheer HIM on. The ball
                     gets to CORTÉZ. CUAUHTÉMOC urges
                     HIM to use HIS forearm in the same
                     way. CORTÉZ hits the ball and misses,
                     the CREW cheering HIM on now. CORTÉZ
                     and CUAUHTÉMOC do this a few times,
                     battling back and forth, until CORTÉZ
                     manages to put the ball through the
                     hoop. AZTECS and CREW cheer and rally
                     behind CORTÉZ.)

                         CUAUHTÉMOC
                       (calculated)
     TO LOSE TO A GOD
     WHEN THE REAL GAME YOU PLAY
     IS SUBTLE AS COPAL
     THAT BURNS WHEN YOU PRAY

     YOU LEAVE ON THE MASK
     YOU GIVE NOTHING AWAY
     UNTIL THE TIME COMES
     TO UNSHEATHE YOUR OBSIDIAN...BLADE!!!

                         CORTÉZ
What now, Marina?

                    MALINALLI
You have won, Hernán.

                    CORTÉZ
Won what?

                    MALINALLI

I--

                    CORTÉZ
              (grabbing HER forcibly)
Answer me!

                    CUAUHTÉMOC
              (to AZTECS)
BRING HIM!!!

              (AZTECS thrust a bound, bloodied
               TOTONAC at CUAUHTÉMOC's feet.
               CUAUHTÉMOC takes HIM by the hair.)

                    CUAUHTÉMOC
              (to CORTÉZ)
YOU'LL RECALL WHEN LAST YOU CAME
WE ROAMED GODLESS AND LOST BY THE LAKE
THEN THE EAGLE DOVE DOWN
AND THE SERPENT HE FOUND
SET THE STAGE
FOR WHAT CAME

FLOWERY WARS WHEN YOU WANTED US TO
BROUGHT BACK PRISONERS BLOODIED AND BRUISED
THEN YOU SHOWED US A GAME
A DANCE OF DEATH WE COULD PLAY
IN YOUR NAME

                    CUAUHTÉMOC & AZTECS
IN YOUR PRAISE!!!

              (CUAUHTÉMOC unsheathes HIS obsidian
               blade.)

                         55

                    CUAUHTÉMOC & AZTECS
NO NEED TO GENUFLECT
SLICE STRAIGHT DOWN FROM THE NECK
THAT IS HOW YOU TAUGHT US
TO EVISCERATE

RIP THE HEART FROM THE CHEST
ONTO SAUCERED INCENSE
AND LEARNING THAT BLOOD LEAVES A STAIN
CUTS JUST LIKE AN OBSIDIAN BLADE

                    CUAUHTÉMOC
DON'T WORRY ABOUT
THE CROWD WATCHING YOU
JUST COME OVER HERE
SHOW US WHAT YOU CAN DO

I'LL HOLD BACK HIS HEAD
WHILE YOU CUT STRAIGHT THROUGH
HE WON'T FEEL A THING
ONCE HIS HEART IS REMOVED

                    (During the next chorus the
                    following occurs: CUAUHTÉMOC offers
                    the blade to CORTÉZ, who accepts it
                    apprehensively. CUAUHTÉMOC waits
                    for CORTÉZ to deal HIS blow. CORTÉZ
                    looks to a wide-eyed MALINALLI;
                    then to JARAMILLO, shaking HIS
                    head; then to ORDAZ and CREW,
                    staring back while fondling the
                    gold and jewels; then to TECUICHPO,
                    still comforting MOCTEZUMA, but
                    curious to see what happens next;
                    and finally to a riveted
                    TEUHTLILTZIN.

                    With the music swelling, CORTÉZ is
                    encroached on both sides by CREW
                    and AZTECS alike, all in a mixture
                    of anxiety, anticipation, and dread
                    as THEY await CORTÉZ's next move.)

                    CUAUHTÉMOC & AZTECS
NO NEED TO GENUFLECT
SLICE STRAIGHT DOWN FROM THE NECK
YOU'RE A GOD
SHOW US HOW YOU EVISCERATE

RIP HIS HEART FROM HIS CHEST
ONTO SAUCERED INCENSE
AND THEN TO THE DOGS WHAT REMAINS
WHEN YOU SLICE WITH OBSIDIAN
CARVE HIM UP WITH OBSIDIAN
SURRENDER TO OBSIDIAN
SACRIFICE WITH OBSIDIAN
BECOME ONE WITH OBSIDIAN BLADE
CUT--HIM--UP!!!

            (TEUHTLILTZIN pulls CORTÉZ from the
             crowd.)

                    TEUHTLILTZIN
LET HIM BE
BE KIND TO OUR GUEST
HE IS TRAVELLED AND WEARY
YET YOU TAUNT HIM THIS WAY

There shall be no sacrifice today. Tecuichpo, take
Quetzalcoatl Cortéz and show him to his temple. I shall
see to the other guests.

                    CUAUHTÉMOC
                   (in protest)
You are not Tlatoani! This is tradition! He will cut this
dog! Right now! Before all of us!
                   (to MOCTEZUMA)
Tetlatzin?

            (MOCTEZUMA fails to respond.)

                    CUAUHTÉMOC
Uncle?!

                    TECUICHPO
I shall take him.

               (Gasps from AZTECS.)

                    CORTÉZ
                 (to MALINALLI)
Why are they arguing? Marina?

               (MALINALLI isn't quick to respond.
                CORTÉZ and Spaniards begin reaching
                for THEIR swords; AZTECS THEIR
                macanas and spears. MALINALLI turns
                to TEUHTLILTZIN, who shakes HIS
                head carefully.)

                    MALINALLI
A god...never dies.

                    CORTÉZ
What?

                    MALINALLI
Forgive me, Hernán.

                    CORTÉZ
You bitch!
                 (rallying Spaniards)
SANTIAGO!

                    CUAUHTÉMOC
                 (rallying AZTECS)
AYYO!

                    TEUHTLILTZIN
NO!

               (CORTÉZ, CREW, and AZTECS draw
                THEIR weapons.)

                    TECUICHPO
Wait!

                    (SHE stands between the two
                    factions.)

                         TECUICHPO
                      (to MOCTEZUMA)
Tahtli, please. Let me go.

                    (MOCTEZUMA looks all around HIM, until
                    the multitude of stares becomes
                    unbearable.)

                         MOCTEZUMA
Do...as Teuhtliltzin says, Daughter.

                    (Mumbles and gasps from the AZTECS.
                    SHE approaches CORTÉZ. SHE motions
                    to AZTECS and THEY lay THEIR
                    weapons down. CORTÉZ motions to HIS
                    men to do the same. TECUICHPO
                    extends HER hand to CORTÉZ. HE
                    hands HER the obsidian blade. SHE
                    offers it back to CUAUHTÉMOC.)

                         CUAUHTÉMOC
                    (taking blade; a capella)
AND WATCHING YOUR LOVE LEAVE THIS STAIN
CUTS JUST LIKE THIS OBSIDIAN BLADE!

                    (HE storms off. Lights change. All
                    exit save TECUICHPO and CORTÉZ.)

22. <u>YOU'RE WHAT I'VE BEEN WAITING FOR</u>

                         CORTÉZ
                    (gazing far and wide)
Astounding. This temple. This city. Everywhere I set my eyes.
What greater grandeur than this?
                    (turning to TECUICHPO)
And you. You saved our lives today. My life. And yet, you do
not understand a single word I am saying.

                    (SHE kneels.)

                         CORTÉZ
                    (stopping HER)
No! No need for that. Show me more.
                         (pointing over Audience)
There. That grand peak, beyond the trees...

                         TECUICHPO
                    (pointing to same spot)
Popocatépetl.

                         CORTÉZ
                    (struggling to pronounce)
Po-po-ca-té-pe-tl.

                         (pointing)
And over there?

                         TECUICHPO
Iztaccíhuatl.

                         CORTÉZ
Iz-tak-sí--Iz-tak-sí--

          (SHE giggles.)

                         CORTÉZ
                    (playfully)
Why, you--

          (HE takes HER by the waist from
           behind; SHE does not resist. THEY
           come together slowly, and both look
           up into the sky.)

                         CORTÉZ
And up there? In your grand, wondrous sky?

                         TECUICHPO
Meztli.

          (SHE turns to face HIM.)

                           60

CORTÉZ

Yes. The moon.

THE TIME IS RIGHT
PERFECT MOONLIGHT
I SEE, STILL I DON'T BELIEVE MY EYES

ON THE BARREN SEAS
WHERE I LOVE TO BE
A MAN GETS LONELY DREAMING
NOW I'VE WOKEN UP TO SEE WHAT I'VE BEEN
MISSING

SOMETHING STRONGER
THAN THE OCEANS I HAVE TRAVELED
SOMETHING STRONGER
THAN THE WINDS

WE ARE STRANGERS
BUT I COULD STAND HERE FOREVER
NEXT TO YOU THERE IS ONE THING THAT I KNOW
YOU'RE WHAT I'VE BEEN WAITING FOR

TECUICHPO

THE TIME IS RIGHT
THE STARS SHINE BRIGHT
THE WHOLE WORLD SLEEPS
BUT YOU AND I

WAS IT FATE
MEETING YOU THIS WAY?
THAT LOVE WOULD COME LIKE THIS?
I YEARN TO FEEL YOUR GENTLE KISS

SOMETHING STRONGER
THAN THE GODS THAT I FOLLOW
SOMETHING STRONGER
THAN THE WINDS

THERE'S A DANGER
EVEN DREAMING OF FOREVER
HERE WITH YOU-STILL THERE'S ONE THING MY HEART KNOWS
YOU'RE WHAT I'VE BEEN WAITING FOR

                              CORTÉZ
I'M EVERYWHERE
JUST STANDING HERE
BREATHING NEXT TO YOU

                         TECUICHPO & CORTÉZ
YOU COULD BE MY DREAM COME TRUE
WHOA
YEAH

              CORTÉZ   TECUICHPO
SOMETHING STRONGER   SOMETHING STRONGER
THAN THE GODS THAT YOU FOLLOW   THAN THE OCEANS YOU HAVE
                                TRAVELLED

                         TECUICHPO & CORTÉZ
SOMETHING STRONGER
THAN THE WINDS
THERE'S A DANGER EVEN DREAMING OF FOREVER
NEXT TO YOU-STILL THERE'S ONE THING MY HEART KNOWS
YOU'RE WHAT I'VE BEEN WAITING FOR
YOU'RE WHAT I'VE BEEN WAITING FOR
YOU'RE WHAT I'VE BEEN WAITING FOR

                    (THEY embrace, kiss, exit in
                     elation. Cloaked and hooded,
                     MALINALLI appears from the shadows,
                     shaken to HER core after what SHE
                     just witnessed.)

23. <u>BETRAYALS</u>

                              MALINALLI
                        (in utter disbelief)
HERNÁN CORTÉZ
YOU'RE IN MY HEAD
I GET THIS FEELING
WHEN I HEAR YOUR NAME

THEN SUDDENLY, I SWEAR
I SEE YOU STANDING THERE
SMILING AT ME

No, Hernán. How could you? After everything…

        (Music changes, reflecting
          MALINALLI's newfound resolve.)

               MALINALLI

HERNÁN CORTÉZ
I CAN'T FORGET
THIS WRONG THAT YOU
HAVE DONE TO ME

NOW LOVE DECAYS TO
HATE FOR YOU INSTEAD
WHEN I THINK ABOUT HERNÁN CORTÉZ
WHEN I THINK ABOUT HERNÁN CORTÉZ
WHEN I THINK ABOUT HERNÁN CORTÉZ

        (MALINALLI rips the rosary from HER
         neck, throws it to the ground, and
         runs off.)

SETTING: That night; MOCTEZUMA's palace.

AT RISE:

>   (MOCTEZUMA sits on HIS throne,
>   Quetzalcoatl's heavy shadow hanging
>   over HIM.)

24. GODS AND MEN

                    MOCTEZUMA
LAST NIGHT THE CHACMOOL SANG A CHORUS
I HEARD WHAT SOUNDED LIKE A NAME
HIS VOICE CAME TO ME FAINT AND POROUS
THEN THE WIND IT DIED
THE WIND IT DIED
AS FIRE RACED ACROSS THE FIRMAMENT
THEN HE LOOKED AT ME AND SAID:
"WELCOME TO THE AGE
OF GODS AND MEN"

LAST NIGHT THE JAGUAR WAS AMONG US
HE PROWLED THE STREETS IN QUIET RAGE
I FOLLOWED HIM INTO THE FOREST
WHERE I SAW HIM CRY
WHERE I WATCHED TWO WORLDS COLLIDE
AS TLALOC'S TEMPLE BURST INTO GREAT FLAME
JUST BEFORE HE CREPT AWAY
HE GROWLED:
"WELCOME TO THE AGE
OF GODS AND MEN"

>   (CUAUHTÉMOC enters.)

                 MOCTEZUMA & CUAUHTÉMOC
GODS AND MEN

>   (TECUICHPO and MALINALLI enter.)

                          MOCTEZUMA, CUAUHTÉMOC, TECUICHPO,
                          & MALINALLI
GODS AND MEN
OH, OH, OH

                          MOCTEZUMA
AND NOW THAT HELLISH
BEATING FROM THOSE DRUMS
AS EACH BRILLIANT STAR FALLS OUT OF THE SKY

                          CUAUHTÉMOC
UNBOUND WHITE DEVILS REVEL IN DISGUISE

                          MOCTEZUMA, CUAUHTÉMOC, TECUICHPO,
                          & MALINALLI
AND THERE IS NO TIME
TO DETERMINE WHAT'S DIVINE

    MOCTEZUMA & MALINALLI   TECUICHPO & CUAUHTÉMOC
AND ALL I ONCE CALLED MINE   AND ALL THAT CAN BE MINE

                          MOCTEZUMA, CUAUHTÉMOC, TECUICHPO,
                          & MALINALLI
IS LOST INSIDE A CRUEL SUNRISE...

                          MOCTEZUMA
LAST NIGHT THE CHACMOOL SANG A CHORUS
I HEARD WHAT SOUNDED LIKE A NAME
HE WHISPERED SOMETHING
FAINT AND DANGEROUS

                          CUAUHTÉMOC, TECUICHPO, & MALINALLI
CORTÉZ...

            (With the weight of HIS world heavy
             upon HIS shoulders, MOCTEZUMA rises.
             HE removes HIS headdress, places it
             on the throne. ALL exit except
             CUAUHTÉMOC.)

25. <u>WORLD OF A DIFFERENCE</u>

>   (Lights change. It is weeks later
>   in the Great Plaza of Tenochtitlán.
>   AZTECS stagger in, struggling to
>   transport gold and jewels to the
>   foot of the throne. THEY all show
>   signs of fatigue, torture, and
>   smallpox. Urging THEM on are ORDAZ,
>   LEÓN, and CREW, all wielding whips
>   as THEY oversee the operation.
>   TEUHTLILTZIN enters, carried on a
>   litter by sickly AZTECS, and
>   donning emperors attire now.
>   TEUHTLILTZIN also exhibits the
>   initial signs of smallpox. Once
>   seated on the throne the AZTECS
>   place the headdress on HIS head.)

                          TEUHTLILTZIN
                       (over music, to Audience,
                        enjoying the show)

And because my father forgot to bury my umbilical cord in
enemy territory, he failed to consecrate me to the warrior's
life. An Eagle Warrior, he did not take it with him into
battle, as he should have done, and it wasn't long before
the gods punished him for his crime. So my mother took me
to see the high priest, where he ground the cord into a
fine powder and gave precise instructions for her to feed
it to me. "Give this to him," he said to her, "and this
child will decide his own fate. This child will decide his
own fate."

                        CREW, ORDAZ, & LEÓN
          HOT FROM THE HEAT OF THE SUN
          BUT STILL WE MELT THEIR IDOLS ONE BY ONE
          TO DISCOURAGE HUMAN SACRIFICE
          AND ALL THEIR OTHER HEATHEN RITES
          THAT IS WHY WE'RE GONNA TAKE IT ALL

                             ORDAZ
                    (striking AZTECS as THEY pass)
¡Rápido!

                    CREW, ORDAZ, & LEÓN
TEOCUITLA-THAT'S THEIR WORD FOR GOLD
THEY CAN'T IMAGINE WHAT WE WANT IT FOR
STILL, WE THINK WE'VE MADE A FAIR EXCHANGE
THEY'RE SET ON KEEPING OUR DISEASES
WHEN WE'VE LEFT THEN THEY CAN FIND A CURE

WE'RE HERE TO MAKE A WORLD OF A DIFFERENCE
WE'RE HERE TO SHOW THEM THAT THERE'S SO MUCH MORE
BUT WE DIDN'T CROSS THE SEA, YOU KNOW
TO GO BACK LIKE WE CAME, THEREFORE
WE DON'T HAVE TIME TO BE THE GODS THEY KNOW
ONLY TO TAKE THE GOLD BACK HOME

                        LEÓN
                  (striking AZTECS)
¡Apúrense!

                  (CORTÉZ and JARAMILLO enter. While
                   CORTÉZ inspects the operation,
                   JARAMILLO's gestures show HIS
                   displeasure at what is transpiring.
                   Spotting HIS nemesis CORTÉZ, LEÓN
                   drops HIS whip, unsheathes HIS sword.)

                        LEÓN
                  (over music, to ORDAZ)
Enough of this! I kill Cortéz, now!

                        ORDAZ
                   (stopping HIM)
No. We agreed: the gold first. Not yet, Juan. Patience.

                        LEÓN
To the hellfires with your patience! Look at him! And all
the while Catalina continues to suffer back home! All this
rage, Diego. What am I do with it?

                        ORDAZ
I'll tell you what.
                        (picking whip up from the
                         ground, digging it into
                         LEÓN's chest)

                         67

Put your sword away, and swallow it!

                        TEUHTLILTZIN
                      (to LEÓN)
Hahaha! Yes, Conquistador. Swallow it. It's not so bad.
Just look at the wonders it's done for me!

                    (HE laughs as Nero did watching
                     Rome burn. LEÓN sheathes HIS sword
                     reluctantly and returns to the work
                     at hand. CORTÉZ and JARAMILLO exit.
                     CUAUHTÉMOC is overcome with rage at
                     the sight of the abuse of HIS
                     people.)

                        CUAUHTÉMOC
     OUR WAY OF LIFE
     IS BEING TORN ASUNDER

                         LEÓN
                    (to AZTECS, no remorse now)
¡Rápido, perros desgraciados!

                        CUAUHTÉMOC
     HOW MUCH LONGER MUST THIS PUNISHMENT GO ON?
     IF GODS ACT DIFFERENTLY THAN MEN
     WHY ARE THEY REJOICING IN
     SEEING ALL THEIR PEOPLE BEATEN DOWN?
     WATCHING AS THEY FALL DEAD TO THE GROUND?

  CREW, TEUHTLILTZIN & AZTECS   CUAUHTÉMOC
WE'RE/THEY'RE HERE TO MAKE A   WHAT WILL HAPPEN TO US
WORLD OF A DIFFERENCE   IF IT ALL GOES THEIR WAY?
TO INTRODUCE THE FATHER, SON   I DON'T KNOW
AND HOLY GHOST

                CREW, TEUHTLILTZIIN, & AZTECS
     WE/THEY BELIEVE THAT YOUR/OUR SALVATION'S
     WORTH
     US/THEM ASSUMING ALL THE LOOT
     MAKING ALL OUR/THEIR DREAMS COME TRUE
     OF COURSE, AT THE EXPENSE OF YOU/US
     A WORLD OF A DIFFERENCE!

                    CUAUHTÉMOC
THIS CAN'T GO ON!

                    CREW, TEUHTLILTZIIN, & AZTECS
A WORLD OF A DIFFERENCE!

                    CUAUHTÉMOC
THE MEXICA ARE STRONG!

                    CREW, TEUHTLILTZIIN, & AZTECS
A WORLD OF A DIFFERENCE FOR SURE

                    CUAUHTÉMOC
THE MEXICA ARE STRONG!

          (Lights change. CREW, AZTECS,
          ORDAZ, and LEÓN exit.)

26. <u>ONE THING I MUST TELL YOU</u>

          (A frail, beleaguered MOCTEZUMA
          enters and stops beside CUAUHTÉMOC.
          MALINALLI enters opposite THEM, cloaked and
          hooded.)

                    MALINALLI
ONE THING I MUST TELL YOU
ONE THING YOU SHOULD KNOW
THOSE WHO CLAIM TO BE GODS
ARE MERE MEN NOTHING MORE

YOU SEE THEY HAVE A DISEASE
THAT ONLY GOLD CAN APPEASE
AND THEY'VE FINALLY FOUND THE CURE

                    TEUHTLILTZIN
WRETCHED WHORE! BITE YOUR TONGUE!
OH, HOW YOU BLASPHEME, MALINCHE!

THEY TAKE GREENSTONES AND GOLD
FOR OUR SOULS THEY PLAN TO SAVE

YOU LED THEM TO OUR DOOR
YOU HELPED CORTÉZ CAJOLE
NOW YOU CHANGE YOUR MIND
DO NOT WASTE OUR TIME
UNLESS…
YOU CAN GIVE US SOMETHING ELSE…

                    MALINALLI
     HERNÁN CORTÉZ-I CAN'T FORGET
     THE WRONG THAT HE HAS DONE TO ME

                    TEUHTLILTZIN
You forget our deal, Malinche!

                    CUAUHTÉMOC
What deal?

                    TEUHTLILTZIN
Guards! Drag her out of here!

                    MALINALLI
Let me show you what I mean.

          (SHE removes HER cloak and exposes
           HER pregnant belly.)

                    MALINALLI
     WITHIN THIS WRETCH
     GROWS THE FIRST OF OUR MIXED RACE
     THE SON OF HERNÁN CORTÉZ!

                    TEUHTLILTZIN
                 (betrayed)
Worthless whore!

          (HE jumps from the throne and
           lunges at MALINALLI, but not before
           CUAUHTÉMOC intercedes. THEY
           struggle until TEUHTLILTZIN loses
           the headdress and escapes.
           MALINALLI also runs off before
           CUAUHTÉMOC can stop HER.)

                    MOCTEZUMA
                 (commanding voice)
Let them go!

                    CUAUHTÉMOC
Uncle, but--

          (HE notices the headdress on the
           ground. HE picks it up carefully,
           presents it to MOCTEZUMA, and
           kneels.)

                    CUAUHTÉMOC
Command me, Tlatoani.

          (MOCTEZUMA dons the headdress.)

                    MOCTEZUMA
                  (reinvigorated)
EVERY MAN MUST MAKE HIS MARK
MAKE HIS STAND OR WHEN HE IS GONE
NO ONE GIVES A DAMN WHO HE WAS
THIS IS MY HOUR-THIS IS MY PART

QUETZALCOATL, YOUR LEGEND ENDS TODAY
BY NOON TOMORROW ONLY YOUR MEMORY WILL
REMAIN

CHOOSE A FEW MEN-NOT A LOT OF THEM
WE'LL STRIKE AT ULUA-DESTROY EVERTHING!
EVERY CRIMSON FLAG! EVERY SPANISH TENT!

                    CUAUHTÉMOC
AYYO!

                MOCTEZUMA & CUAUHTÉMOC
IN EVERY MAN'S LIFE THERE COMES A DECISION
THE ONE THAT WILL CHANGE IT ALL FOREVER
THIS IS THE MOMENT WE RECLAIM PATRIMONY
ON THIS NIGHT

                        71

THE GODS WILL BLEED!

(THEY exit.)

SCENE 3

SETTING: Evening of June 30, 1520;
                                            a Garden in Tenochtitlán

AT RISE:

                    (Lights change. Hand in hand,
                 CORTÉZ and TECUICHPO enter.)

27. <u>LA NOCHE TRISTE</u>

CORTÉZ
HERE WE ARE AGAIN, YOU AND I, FACE TO FACE
WHILE THE WORLD ALL AROUND US SLOWLY TURNS
I SEE YOU SMILE AND THAT'S ALL YOU NEED TO DO

THEN SOMEWHERE IS HERE
WHERE YOU ARE…

Come, you must show me more!
                            (pointing)
That gárgola-like statue, there?

TECUICHPO
Chacmool.

CORTÉZ
Amazing! And that? It dwarfs even the greatest olive trees
in Medellin. Its name?

TECUICHPO
Ahuehuete.

CORTÉZ
Wonderful! Your words! This world!
                    (caressing HER face)
It doesn't get better than this.

                    (SHE blushes, then remembers that
                     special something SHE found along

73

the way: the remnants of
MALINALLI's rosary.)

                    CORTÉZ
                 (playfully)
And what do you have there? Come now, what is it?

          (SHE gladly shows it to HIM. HE
            recognizes the rosary immediately.)

                    CORTÉZ
Where did you find this?
                    (beat, in sudden rage)
How did you get this?

          (SHE pulls away, falls to the
            ground, scared and confused.)

                    CORTÉZ
                 (remembering MALINALLI;
                  slowly and a capella)
    SOMEWHERE
    SOMEWHERE SHE MUST BE ALONE AND WONDERING WHY
    I ONLY CHOSE TO HOLD HER IN MY ARMS THOSE NIGHTS

    I DON'T KNOW WHERE YOU ARE
    NEAR OR FAR...

          (LEÓN enters with sword drawn, a
            determined look on HIS face.)

                    CORTÉZ
León, I gave strict orders to be left alone.
                    (Beat.)
Why do you come to me with a drawn sword?

                    LEÓN
    AT LAST, ALONE WITHIN MY GRASP
    YOUR PRIDE OF STONE I WILL BREAK FAST
    YOUR DREAMS, YOUR HOPES WILL NEVER COME TO PASS
    AT LAST, YOU'LL DIE FOR ALL MY PAST

Time to settle our debt, Hernán.

                    CORTÉZ
What are you talking about?

                    LEÓN
Catalina, you fool! She suffers back home when she should
have married me.

            (TECUICHPO attempts to rise; CORTÉZ
            motions for HER to stay where SHE
            is.)

                    LEÓN
Ha! And what is this? Your new Indian whore? And this one
the monarch's daughter?
                    (to TECUICHPO)
Get out of here, witch! Unless you wish to die alongside
him!

                    CORTÉZ
    WE STAND AMIDST THE GREATEST CITY
    OUR EYES, THE WORLD HAS EVER KNOWN
    YOU COME TO ME WITH LOST LOVE STORIES
    DO WHAT YOU WILL!
    DO WHAT YOU WILL!

            (HE draws HIS sword. ORDAZ and
            JARAMILLO enter.)

                    ORDAZ
León, no!

                    JARAMILLO
Hernán!

                    LEÓN & CORTÉZ
    YES I KNOW
    I AM GIVING UP MY SOUL IN THIS ENDEAVOR
    MORE THAN GOLD
    ARE THE CONTOURS OF HER EYES TO ME
    DAMNED I MAY BE

FOLLOWING THIS DREAM
BUT THAT'S ALL THE HEAVEN I NEED!

      (Just as LEÓN and CORTÉZ crash
      swords, MOCTEZUMA, CUAUHTÉMOC, and
      AZTECS attack. CUAUHTÉMOC strikes
      LEÓN dead, then duels with
      JARAMILLO. ORDAZ fends off AZTECS
      as best HE can, but is eventually
      overtaken and killed. In fury,
      MOCTEZUMA aims straight for CORTÉZ,
      unleashing a series of strikes that
      force CORTÉZ to the ground. Just as
      MOCTEZUMA is about to deal the
      final blow, TECUICHPO cuts between
      THEM. MOCTEZUMA is thunderstruck.
      In overwhelming rage, HE prepares
      to strike THEM both down.
      JARAMILLO, meanwhile, manages to
      fend off CUAUHTÉMOC. Before
      MOCTEZUMA's stroke falls, JARAMILLO
      plunges HIS sword into HIM.)

        TECUICHPO   CUAUHTÉMOC
No!!!   Uncle!!!

        MOCTEZUMA
        (to JARAMILLO)
Tonatiuh...
Tonatiuh...

      (HE falls to the ground, dead.)

        TECUICHPO
      (rushing to MOCTEZUMA)
Tahtli!!!

      (CUAUHTÉMOC rips TECUICHPO from HER
      dead father and THEY retreat.)

      (Lights dim. JARAMILLO hangs over
      MOCTEZUMA's corpse.)

28. THE SONG WILL GO ON

JARAMILLO

I LOOK AT YOU AND SEE
A BROKEN KING LOOKING AT ME
REACHING OUT WITH ONCE-PROUD HANDS
AND ASKING ME TO SET HIM FREE

AS YOU LAY THERE ALL ALONE
WONDERING WHERE IT ALL WENT WRONG
SILENT IN YOUR FATAL STANCE

I'D REVIVE YOU IF I COULD
BUT WOULD IT DO ANY GOOD
WHEN ALL OF YOUR PEOPLE
HAVE LOST THEIR FAITH IN YOU?

I COULD LET LOOSE DEATH'S CRUEL CHAIN
AND STILL YOUR PRISON WOULD REMAIN
IF ONLY YOU HAD NOT LET US PASS
NOW THERE'S NO TURNING BACK

NOW THE SONG WILL GO ON
LEAVING YOU WITH NO CHOICE
BUT TO SING ALONG

WHAT YOU HAD IN YOUR HANDS
IS GONE NOW-FADED AWAY
AND TO THINK I PLAYED A PART
FRIGHTENS ME…

I STILL HAVEN'T FORGOTTEN
WHAT JUST NOW YOU FIRST CALLED ME
"TONATIUH," THAT MEANS THE SUN
HOW WRONG COULD YOU BE?

FOR I HAVE BROUGHT THE SUN
DOWN ON YOUR KINGDOM NOW, IT SEEMS
WITH NO CHANCE FOR A NEW DAWN
OR ANY NEW BEGINNINGS

I CURSE THE DAY

I CHOSE TO COME
AND THE DAY I MADE THE PROMISE
TO SEE IT ALL DONE

WHEN CORTÉZ CHOSE TO MARCH
TO TENOCHTITLÁN
NOW TELL ME
WHAT DO YOU THINK OF YOUR SUN?

                    CHORUS & JARAMILLO
NOW THE SONG WILL GO ON
LEAVING YOU/ME WITH NO CHOICE
BUT TO SING ALONG

WHAT YOU/I HAD IN YOUR/MY HANDS
IS GONE NOW-FADED AWAY
AND TO THINK WE/I PLAYED A PART
AND WE/I TORE YOUR DREAMS APART
COULD YOU FIND IT IN YOUR HEART
TO FORGIVE US/ME
OH, OH, OH

FORGIVE US/ME
OH, OH, OH, OH, OH
OH!!!

            (Blackout.)

            (Lights rise on a barren stage.
             TECUICHPO reappears opposite a
             large-bellied MALINALLI.)

29. <u>IN HIS ARMS</u>

                    TECUICHPO
I HAVE A PICTURE IN MY MIND
OF THE WAY HE IS
AND EVERYTHING INSIDE IS TELLING ME
THAT IS HOW HE'S ALWAYS BEEN

OH, EVERY MEMORY BY HIS SIDE
TAKES THE LONELINESS WITHIN ME

TRANSPORTS ME TO THAT TIME
WHEN IN HIS ARMS I LAY IN HIS EMBRACE

                    MALINALLI

IN HIS ARMS
EVERYTHING WAS RIGHT
HE WAS REAL
AND SO WAS LOVE

                    TECUICHPO

IN HIS ARMS
I COULD CLOSE MY EYES
JUST TO FEEL
HIS GENTLE TOUCH

                    MALINALLI

IN HIS ARMS
THE ONLY DANGER
WAS FALLING
DEEPER IN LOVE

                    TECUICHPO

IN HIS ARMS
I FELT SOMETHING STRONGER
THAN ALL I'D EVER
DREAMED OF

                TECUICHPO & MALINALLI

HOLDING ME TIGHT
LOOKING IN HIS EYES
I'D KNOW
IN HIS ARMS

                    MALINALLI
CAN'T GET HIM OUT OF MY HEAD

                    TECUICHPO
CAN'T FORGET HERNÁN CORTÉZ

                    MALINALLI
THOSE BURNING NIGHTS IN HIS BED
                    (looking down, caressing belly)

YOU'RE ALL I'LL HAVE OF THOSE FEW NIGHTS

                        TECUICHPO
I STILL REMEMBER EVERY NIGHT

                        TECUICHPO & MALINALLI
HE IS THE DREAM THAT
BURNS INSIDE MY MIND

                        TECUICHPO

IN HIS ARMS
THE ONLY DANGER
WAS FALLING
DEEPER IN LOVE

                        MALINALLI

IN HIS ARMS
I FELT SOMETHING STRONGER
THAN ALL I'D EVER DREAMED OF

                        TECUICHPO & MALINALLI

HOLDING HIM TIGHT
LOOKING IN HIS EYES

                        TECUICHPO

I'D LET GO

                        MALINALLI
                  (to belly)
SOMEDAY YOU WILL KNOW

                        TECUICHPO & MALINALLI
HOW I TOUCHED THE STARS
IN HIS ARMS

                  (Enter CUAUHTÉMOC, dressed in
                   emperors attire now, and donning
                   MOCTEZUMA's headdress. HE crosses
                   to a downcast TECUICHPO.)

                        80

CUAUHTÉMOC
(slowly, a capella)
AND LEARNING THAT BLOOD LEAVES A STAIN...

I told you...

YOU WOULD LOVE ME!

> (HE extends HIS hand. A sigh of
> defeat from TECUICHPO. SHE takes
> HIS hand as HE escorts HER
> offstage.)

30. TLAKATILISTLI (THE BIRTH)

> (Lights change. MALINALLI staggers
> downstage center as labor pains
> begin to overtake HER. SHE falls
> to the ground, cries, writhes in the
> pain of child birth. The music
> reaches a climax, and MALINALLI
> gives out one final, powerful cry.
> The music stops suddenly.
>
> The cry of the first mestizo--a
> child of both Indigenous
> and Spanish blood--resounds.)

MALINALLI
(to child, over music)
You are the painful birth. You are my eagle. My jaguar. My
ocelot. My son. My beautiful son...

31. JAGUAR AND OCELOT

> (Lights turn sinister. TEUHTLILTZIN
> stumbles in painfully. HE shows
> signs of advanced small pox now,
> HIS body covered almost entirely in
> boils. MALINALLI pulls HER child
> close.)

81

                    TEUHTLILTZIN
I REMEMBER EVERY SCHEME
HOW PERFECT THEY ALL SEEMED
WITH YOU TO SEE THEM THROUGH
NOTHING ELSE COULD COME BETWEEN

IN A FLASH IT ALL WENT WRONG
IN A FLASH IT ALL WAS GONE

          (HE coughs painfully.)

                    TEUHTLILTZIN
SIX MONTHS HAVE COME AND GONE
SINCE CORTÉZ WAS DRIVEN OUT
BUT HE'S LINGERED ON THE SHORE
MAKING FRIENDS WITHOUT A DOUBT

WHILE CUAUHTÉMOC SITS AND WAITS
PLANNING STEPS THAT HE WILL TAKE
WHEN THE SPANIARDS COME AGAIN
AND HE THINKS THAT HE CAN WIN

NOW THE SONG WILL GO ON
BUT NOT FOR LONG
THIS IS NOT WHAT I WANTED
AFTER COMING SO FAR

WHAT WE HAD IN OUR HANDS
IS GONE NOW-FADED AWAY
AND TO THINK YOU PLAYED A PART
INFURIATES ME…

A god never dies, Malinche. You swore! Now, look at me!

                    MALINALLI
He betrayed us first!

                    TEUHTLILTZIN
You deserve nothing, not even his bastard son.
                    (approaching menacingly)
Give him to me!

                    MALINALLI
                    (rising)
You will not touch him!

                        TEUHTLILTZIN

I will end you both!

                          MALINALLI

No! He will outlive us all and everything we have done!
You will not have him!

                        TEUHTLILTZIN

Yes I will!!!

                    (Before HE can lunge at HER,
                     MOCTEZUMA's ghost appears, stopping
                     TEUHTLILTZIN in HIS tracks.)

                        TEUHTLILTZIN
                        (with dread)
          MOCTEZUMA, BELIEVE ME
          IT WOULD NOT HAVE COME TO THIS
          IF CORTÉZ HAD HEEDED WORDS
          INSTEAD OF LOVER'S DREAMS

          IF MALINCHE HADN'T SEEN
          CORTÉZ LOST WITHIN A KISS
          I WOULD BE EMPEROR
          AND NOW WE WOULD HAVE PEACE

                    (The macabre Tzompantli, the
                     infamous Skull Rack of
                     Tenochtitlán, appears in the
                     background. AZTECS, NOBLES, and
                     CREW enter, THEIR faces ghostly,
                     THEIR bodies in decay. THEY
                     encroach TEUHTLILTZIN from all
                     sides. MOCTEZUMA reveals an
                     obsidian blade, starts towards
                     TEUHTLILTZIN.)

                        TEUHTLILTZIN

          BUT NOW THE JAGUAR
          AND THE OCELOT
          PREPARE FOR
          THEIR ATTACK

          AND THEY HUNGER
          FOR THE CHANCE

TO TAKE ALL
I HAVE LEFT

AND AS MY SPEARS
LIE BROKEN
IN BLOOD-SOAKED
SPANISH FLAGS

>   (MOCTEZUMA offers HIM the blade.
>   Surrounded by ghosts,
>   TEUHTLILTZIN sees no other choice
>   but to take it.)

                         TEUHTLILTZIN
THE WORLD OF THE MEXICA
WILL CRUMBLE AWAY
THE FOUNDATION STONES
OF OUR PYRAMIDS RAZED

AND TEZCATLIPOCA WILL
SET DOWN HIS GAZE
UPON DESOLATION
WHERE I USED TO REIGN

MOCTEZUMA
WILL THE FAULT BE MINE?
TENOCHTITLÁN

Fine!!!

>   (HE plunges the blade into HIS
>   chest, dies. Blackout save for
>   spotlight on MALINALLI.)

32. OLLINTONATIUH (FIFTH SUN)

>   (Lights rise slowly with the music
>   to reveal Tenochtitlán in ruins.
>   Scattered across the stage lie
>   CREW, NOBLES and AZTECS, bloodied
>   and languishing in defeat and
>   disease. As MALINALLI staggers into
>   this, THEY reach out to HER and the

child, then die one by one. Surrounded
by nothing but death and destruction,
SHE does not look away or cower in
fear, and each step SHE takes seems
to strengthen HER resolve to keep
moving.

SHE meanders to JARAMILLO downstage
as the music ends. Bruised from battle,
the Spaniard stands over TECUICHPO who
has died from smallpox.)

                    JARAMILLO
                (noticing MALINALLI)
You? By God, why have you come back here?
                (noticing the child)
What is this?

                    MALINALLI
                (firmly)
Where is he, Juan?

                    JARAMILLO
Get out of here!

                    MALINALLI
I will not. Where is he?

                    JARAMILLO
He will kill you. The child as well. Go!

                    MALINALLI
No! He will see him! He must see him! Where is he?

            (CORTÉZ hulks in, battle-scarred, a
            bloodied sword in hand, leading
            CUAUHTÉMOC in chains.)

                    CORTÉZ
Juan!
                (Beat.)
Step away.

                    (CUAUHTÉMOC notices TECUICHPO'S
                    body, runs to HER, falls to HIS
                    knees.)

                         CORTÉZ
                   (a cappella, with a lump in
                    HIS throat, as CUAUHTÉMOC
                    agonizes)
            HERE WE ARE AGAIN
            FACE TO FACE
            WHILE THE WORLD AROUND US
            SLOWLY BURNS...
                      (looking to TECUICHPO, but
                      menacingly to MALINALLI)
Give me one reason not to strike you down, Malinche. Here and
now! For all you've done!

                    (SHE uncovers the child.)

                         CORTÉZ
I see. Is that what you've been doing all this time?

                         MALINALLI
Look at him!

                         CORTÉZ
Never.

                         MALINALLI
Look at him, Hernán! Know his face, before you never set
eyes on him again!

                    (CUAUHTÉMOC cries.)

                         MALINALLI
                      (still to CORTÉZ)
You chose her, and now her kingdom is destroyed.
                      (looking at child)
Me, I choose him. And I will show him what I know best--I
will teach him to survive. He will never know your name, but
all will fear him. You will fill your ships with gold and
riches, but he will rule these lands long after you are gone.

                            86

                    CORTÉZ
Will he?

                    MALINALLI
I promise you. Now take your city. But get out of our way.

                    CORTÉZ
As you wish.

              (HE steps back to let HER through.
              As SHE passes HIM, HE wrests the
              child from HER. JARAMILLO takes
              hold of MALINALLI.)

                    MALINALLI
You vipers! He is mine! My child! Give him back to me!

                    CORTÉZ
              (staring at child but to
              JARAMILLO)
Juan!

                    JARAMILLO
Capitán!

                    CORTÉZ
You heard what she just said: The city is ours.

                    MALINALLI
Let me go!

                    CORTÉZ
See to the wounded...

                    MALINALLI
No, Hernán! Don't do this!

                    CORTÉZ
              (eyes stabbing HER)
Then burn it all down to the ground!

                         JARAMILLO
                        (conflicted)
As...you wish, Capitán.

                    (CORTÉZ stomps off.)

                         MALINALLI
NO!!! HERNÁN! NO!!!

                    (SHE screams in a desperation, rage
                     and agony that echoes through Space
                     and Time. SHE breaks away from
                     JARAMILLO and falls to HER knees
                     centerstage.)

33. <u>GODDESS (FINALE)</u>

                    (The background transforms into
                     twin pyramids that intersect to
                     form the letter M, symbolic of the
                     legacies prescribed to MALINALLI
                     through the ages--honorable and
                     horrible--including Motherhood,
                     Mestizaje, Memory, even
                     Monstrosity.)

                    (The ghosts of TEUHTLILTZIN and
                     MOCTEZUMA enter opposite each
                     other. TEUHTLILTZIN carries the
                     child before HIM; MOCTEZUMA HIS
                     headdress.)

                         TEUHTLILTZIN
                        (delivering child to
                         MALINALLI)
THEY'LL SAY YOU BETRAYED YOUR PEOPLE
THEY'LL SAY YOU'RE THE ONE TO BLAME

                         MOCTEZUMA
                        (placing headdress on
                         MALINALLI)
THAT YOU ADDED INJURY TO INSULT
WHEN THE SPANIARDS CAME

(The ghosts of ORDAZ and LEÓN
    enter.)

ORDAZ & LEÓN
THEY'LL SAY THAT YOU BROUGHT THE END
WHEN YOU MADE CORTÉZ YOUR FRIEND

JARAMILLO
THAT YOU OFFERED HIM YOUR HAND
WHILE WE CRUSHED TENOCHTITLÁN

(The rest of the dead resurrect and
    join in song. CUAUHTÉMOC rises and
    breaks free from HIS chains.)

COMPANY
AH, AH, AH, AH, AH, AH, AH
AH, AH, AH, AH, AH, AH, AH

CUAUHTÉMOC
YOU KNOW, YOU COULD HAVE BEEN A PRINCESS
BUT YOUR FATHER DIED FIGHTING THE AZTECS

TECUICHPO
THEN YOUR MOTHER CHOSE A MAN
HAD A SON AND YOU WERE SHUNNED AWAY

MALINALLI
WHEN YOUR MOTHER GIVES YOU AWAY
AND YOU GET SOLD OFF AS A SLAVE
THEN CORTÉZ ARRIVES
TAKES YOU IN HIS STRIDE
AND YOU HELP HIM COMMUNICATE
UNTIL LOVE GETS IN THE WAY

JUST LIKE THE GODDESS
CUT INTO PIECES
YOU'RE ROBBED OF ALL THAT IS DIVINE
FOR JUST THE CRIME OF BEING BORN

JUST LIKE THE GODDESS
WON'T RULE OUT VENGEANCE

89

```
YOU GIRD YOUR DREAMS
AND BIDE YOUR TIME
UNTIL THE DAY YOU WILL TRANSFORM
INTO THE GODDESS

        (Cast spreads out to form the
         letter M, with MALINALLI positioned
         at the center tip.)

                    MALINALLI
HISTORY YOU ARE THE LIES
THAT MEN HAVE WROUGHT
CORTÉZ SAILED OFF WITH THE SPOILS
BUT IT WAS I WHO WON

I GAZED WITH LOVE AT
THE SERPENT'S TENDER FACE
I PAID THE PRICE FOR US ALL
THE NEW COSMIC RACE

OH, NOW I HAUNT THROUGH SPACE AND TIME
                 (looking at child)
NOW AS I GAZE INTO YOUR EYES

        (SHE is wrapped in a beautiful blue-
         green coat decorated with small
         golden stars. ALL kneel before
         MALINALLI.)
```

MALINALLI	COMPANY
JUST LIKE THE GODDESS	MOTHER OF MÉXICO
CUT INTO PIECES	MONSTER AND METAPHOR
WE GATHER ALL THAT IS DIVINE	MARTÍN CORTÉZ
LIMBS, HEART AND SOUL	MESTIZO
WE ARE REBORN	
	MOTHER OF MÉXICO
JUST LIKE THE GODDESS	MONSTER AND METAPHOR
NOT LIKE YOUR JESUS	MARTÍN CORTÉZ
WE DEAL THE WRATH INSIDE THE	MESTIZO
STORM	
WE ARE MALINCHE, BUT	
TRANSFORMED	
INTO THE GODDESS	GODDESS...
BEWARE THE GODDESS	GODDESS...

           (MALINALLI holds the child up high,
           the letter M on his chest.)

                 MALINALLI & COMPANY
WE ARE THE GODDESS!

         (Curtain.)

             END OF ACT II

Malinalli

Musical Selections

Zenzontle

Music and Lyrics by Robert Paul Moreira

Piano Arrangement by Josiah David Esquivel

Zenzontle

Zenzontle

A-ny sound is fine   A-ny sound will do   A - ny sound is

fine

Promises

Music and lyrics by Robert Paul Moreira

Piano Arrangements by Josiah David Esquivel

ORDAZ:
My friend I know what you yearn to do___ I see the ven - geance in your eyes

I for - e - ver will stand by your side___ but we must bide our time___

ORDAZ: All I'm a-sking is for some time __ We will both make sure he dies __

But not yet When the time is right __ Will you change your

(JARAMILLO enters.)

JARAMILLO: Her-

mind? nán do you rea-lize what this means? This chan-ges e-very-thing we came here for

CORTÉZ:
See the pos-si-bi-li-ties of what I have in mind

Is this trea-son worth its weight in gold?
Oh, no, no,

We have the chance of a life - time here____ My mi-ssion now is all too clear

no
No, Her - nán, no ____

(Under Dialogue)
CORTÉZ: Can I count on you, Juan?

JARAMILLO: I don't know. I just don't know...

♩. = 60

Promises

Promises

COMPANY:

In e-very one's life there comes a de-ci-sion The one that will change it

all for-ever____ This is the mo-ment we mark u-pon his-to-ry

CORTÉZ
MOCTEZUMA:

(MALINALLI finally places the helmet on CORTÉZ's head.
The CREW and AZTECS cheer "Santiago!" and "Ayyo!" respectively.)

Will you stand by me?____

COMPANY:

Pro-mi-ses pro-mi-ses some-times are trea-cher-ous Still we must go our own way____ When

Ollintonatuih

Fifth Sun

Music by Josiah David Esquivel

Ollintonatuih (Fifth Sun)

Author Biographies

ROBERT PAUL MOREIRA teaches fiction and playwriting at the University of Texas Rio Grande Valley in Edinburg, Texas. He is the editor of *¡Arriba Baseball!: A Collection of Latino Baseball Fiction* and *Scores*, winner of the 2016 NACCS Tejas FOCO Fiction Award. In addition to *Malinalli*, his plays include *Roses From Castile* and *Miriam's Song*. Currently, he is editing a Covid-themed anthology of short plays with playwright Philip Zwerling. The anthology will be published by FlowerSong Press in Fall 2022. For more on Robert and his work, visit www.robertpaulmoreira.com.

JOSIAH ESQUIVEL is a composer, arranger, and guitarist. He holds a BA in Music, focusing on guitar performance and composition, from the University of Texas Rio Grande Valley. A two-time Engaged Scholar awardee, Josiah has composed works for guitar, voice, piano and mixed ensembles. Past theatrical show collaborations include *Bonnie and Clyde*, *In The Heights*, *Rock of Ages*, and *The Best Little Whorehouse in Texas*. As *Malinalli* co-composer, he's also held a variety of additional roles throughout the workshop process, including transcriber, musical director, arranger, orchestrator, and musician. His EP of original music, *C- He-Mc-Al*, is available on SoundCloud, and he is currently developing his own original musical.

www.ingramcontent.com/pod-product-compliance
Lightning Source LLC
Chambersburg PA
CBHW081002140626
46546CB00018B/2958